Sales Technology

Sales Technology

Making the Most of Your Investment

Nikolaos G. Panagopoulos, PhD

First published in 2010 by
Business Expert Press, LLC
222 East 46th Street, New York, NY 10017
www.businessexpertpress.com

ISBN-13: 978-1-60649-116-4 (paperback)
ISBN-10: 1-60649-116-4 (paperback)

ISBN-13: 978-1-60649-117-1 (e-book)
ISBN-10: 1-60649-117-2 (e-book)

DOI 10.4128/9781606491171

A publication in the Business Expert Press Selling and Sales Force Management collection

Collection ISSN: Forthcoming (print)
Collection ISSN: Forthcoming (electronic)

Cover design by Jonathan Pennell
Interior design by Scribe, Inc.

First edition: July 2010

10 9 8 7 6 5 4 3 2 1

Printed in the United States of America.

*To my father and mother
for giving me the most precious of all gifts: life.*

Abstract

Contemporary sales organizations are spending billions of dollars or euros on sales technologies with the objective of streamlining the sales process, enhancing sales force productivity, and improving customer relationships. A variety of sales technologies exist such as customer relationship management (CRM) software, mobile sales force automation (SFA) applications, contact management software, and territory planning applications, to name just a few. In spite of the amount being invested in such technologies, however, few firms can claim to be enjoying performance improvements. In fact, the majority of companies are struggling to gain salesperson buy-ins and are failing to realize the intended return on investment (ROI). In addition, the introduction of such technological applications may cause stress to the sales force or disturb customer relationships. Against this backdrop, this textbook is concerned with how executives can effectively manage a complex and costly sales technology initiative in order to get the most out of it. In particular, the textbook begins by providing the reader with a detailed discussion on the various technologies that are being used by sales organizations. It then provides an exhaustive review of the factors that might lead to effective sales technology implementation and presents a managerially relevant conceptual framework, which illuminates the mediating pathways from using the system to salesperson productivity. Moreover, the textbook offers a wide array of key performance indicators (KPIs) that can be readily employed in order to monitor the progress and success of the implementation effort. Next, it offers a comprehensive method that executives can use to calculate the return on sales technology investment (ROSTI) in order to substantiate the business case for the technology. Finally, the textbook provides executives with a detailed three-stage process of sales technology implementation and discusses what essential work should be conducted in each stage.

Keywords

Customer relationship management (CRM), sales force automation (SFA), sales technology, automation, information technology, salesperson, performance, productivity, implementation, sales force, adoption, customer relationships, return on investment

Contents

Structure of the Book

The past three decades have been characterized by a rapid growth in the domain of information and communication technologies, which are increasingly becoming less expensive and more easy to use. A direct consequence of these evolutions is the breadth and capabilities of applications that these technologies are finding in the functioning of contemporary organizations. Given the fundamental importance of the sales organization for the prosperity and growth of any business-to-business organization, it is not surprising that the sales function has been largely affected by the introduction of such technologies. In fact, contemporary sales organizations are spending billions of dollars and euros on sales technologies with the objective of learning more about their customers, streamlining sales processes, and enhancing sales force performance. A variety of sales technologies exist, such as customer relationship management (CRM) software and suites, mobile sales force automation (SFA) applications, contact management software, SaaS (software-as-a-service), and territory planning applications, to name just a few.

In spite of the amounts being invested in, and the attention being paid to, sales technologies, however, few organizations can claim to be enjoying performance improvements. Most are struggling to gain salesperson buy-in and are failing to realize the intended return on investment.[1] In addition, the introduction of such technological applications may cause stress to the sales force and disturb customer relationships. As such, it comes as no surprise that less than 40% of the firms implementing such systems realize adoption rates above 90%,[2] and that nearly 30% of firms have users who spend very little time, if any at all, using technology solutions.[3] But why do so many firms around the world confront so many difficulties during sales technology implementation, and how can firms get the most out of their investments? Academics and practitioners seem to agree that failure is rarely contingent on the technology itself;

rather, it is contingent on the managerial process employed to implement the technology.[4]

Against this background, this book's primary objective is to provide a comprehensive understanding of sales technology implementation, and to aid organizations in effectively managing a complex and costly sales technology initiative in order to get the most out of it. To achieve its objective, the book draws not only on extant academic research but also on relevant practitioner literature in order to effectively blend theory with practice.

Naturally, this book targets the following four audiences:

1. Executives in adopting firms charged with the difficult task of implementing sales technology
2. Executives in vendor firms aiming at enhancing effective implementation of their solutions within client firms
3. SFA/CRM consulting agencies
4. Students taking an advanced sales management course

The book begins by providing the reader with a detailed discussion of the various technologies that are being used by sales organizations and by providing a brief historical overview of how sales technologies have evolved (chapter 1). It then outlines a process of sales technology implementation and distills the practitioner and academic literature to delineate the factors that can lead to effective sales technology acceptance and usage (chapters 2 and 3). Next, it discusses how sales technologies can impact salesperson performance (chapter 4), and then presents a set of relevant key performance indicators, as well as a managerial method, that executives can use to calculate the performance impacts of technology investments (chapter 5). Finally, it provides executives with a set of managerially relevant guidelines regarding how sales technology implementations should be managed in order to gain the most from such an investment (chapter 6).

Acknowledgments

I would like to thank Michael Ahearne and Adam Rapp (coeditors) for kindly inviting me to write this book and for their feedback on a previous draft.

CHAPTER 1

Sales Technologies

Their Definition, History, and Uses

Chapter Overview

The aim of this chapter is to introduce readers to the various notions and concepts related to sales technologies. In particular the chapter starts with defining sales technology, sales force automation (SFA), and customer relationship management (CRM), and delineates the similarities and differences between these concepts. Likewise, it examines CRM from both a technological and a strategic perspective. This is done in order to set out the boundaries of the topics examined in this book. Next, the chapter proceeds by giving a historical presentation of how sales technologies have evolved, from early applications to modern Internet-based solutions. This is followed by an effort to set out the various types of sales technologies, based on their usage by different constituencies and the type of the selling context they are involved in. The chapter concludes with a brief reference to the world market of sales technologies.

Defining Sales Technology

Rapid changes occurring in the field of information and communication technologies are changing the way society, in general, and business organizations, in specific, organize themselves. These changes have magnified the availability of information in such a way that managers can have immediate access to almost any piece of information needed in order to make better decisions. As such, it is not surprising that several authors have long been contemplating that the ability of accessing, managing, and exploiting information represents an asset of critical importance for the success of the modern firm[1] and for the development of competitive advantage.[2] The importance of information for contemporary organizations is largely driven by the intensified competition in many markets around the world, as well as by increases in customer demands for faster and better service through the provision of customized solutions.

Generally speaking, technology can be defined as "the process of managing the uncertainty and risk surrounding the transactions necessary to convert inputs into output."[3] This rather broad definition refers to any technology (process or administrative technology) employed by organizations in order to manage business processes, such as supply chain, financial management, and production. Given the focus of this book, however, two broad types of technology—namely, information systems (IS) and information technology (IT)—are of special interest to us. Though no clear distinction between the two types of technology is made in the literature, IS usually refers to the software applications and databases, whereas IT refers to a broad spectrum of devices, hardware, and media used by organizations in order to link IS with employees and organizational processes.[4]

Though satisfying diverse customer needs and demands should be a firmwide priority, the sales function of business-to-business organizations plays a prominent role in this process. This is so because the sales function is closer to customers than any other business function, and thus can significantly affect the process of providing services, goods, and solutions. As such, many authors have expressed the sentiment that the use of information and communication technologies can positively contribute to the sales function's effort of satisfying customer needs.[5] Given the critical role of sales for developing intimate and profitable relationships with customers, as well as its impact on net revenues, it is of little wonder that firms have found themselves rushing to invest in sales technologies. Indeed, according to recent reports, the estimated worldwide investment for purchasing CRM software is around $9–11 billion.[6]

Taking a broader view, sales technology can be defined as any information and communication technology employed by the sales organization to conduct its essential activities.[7] However, despite their wide application in modern organizations, sales technologies can mean different things to different constituents. The most commonly encountered confusion regards the identification of sales technology with such concepts as CRM and SFA. Therefore, the purpose of this section is to elaborate on the various terms, which are frequently used interchangeably, and present their differences and similarities. To facilitate comparison among the various terms, Table 1.1 lists a representative set of definitions presented in the literature that can be used to illustrate the different perspectives adopted to study SFA, CRM, and sales technologies.

A careful observation of Table 1.1 reveals that no general agreement exists regarding these terms. SFA, for instance, has been defined in a variety of ways. One common theme underlying all definitions, however, is

Table 1.1. A Variety of Perspectives on the Domains of SFA, CRM, and Sales Technologies

Sales force automation (SFA)
"SFA systems consist of centralized database systems that can be accessed through a modem by remote laptop computers using special SFA software (which is often company specific)."[8]
"SFA involves converting manual sales activities to electronic processes through the use of various combinations of hardware and software applications."[9]
"Adding technology in the form of cellular phones, faxes, portable computers, databases, the Internet, and electronic data interchange (EDI) systems to the sales process."[10]
"Sales force automation (SFA) refers to the use of computer hardware, software, and telecommunications devices by salespeople in their selling and/or administrative activities . . . the SFA system integrates its various activities and applications to support one overriding goal: enhancement of the collection, assimilation, analysis, and distribution of information to improve productivity of the sales force, while enhancing customer relationships."[11]
"Technology for SFA involves a variety of hardware and software capabilities and can support cost reduction or emphasize gains in customer relationship management."[12]
"Laptop computer-based systems that connect via modem to a central server allowing for communication between all parties throughout the country."[13]
"Sales force automation (SFA) occurs when firms computerize routine tasks or adopt technological tools to improve the efficiency or precision of sales force activities."[14]
Customer relationship management (CRM)
"[A] process that addresses all aspects of identifying customers, creating customer knowledge, building customer relationships, and shaping their perceptions of the organization and its products."[15]
"We define the CRM process at the customer-facing level as a systematic process to manage customer relationship initiation, maintenance, and termination across all customer contact points to maximize the value of the relationship portfolio."[16]
"An ongoing process that involves the development and leveraging of market intelligence for the purpose of building and maintaining a profit-maximizing portfolio of customer relationships."[17]

Table 1.1. A Variety of Perspectives on the Domains of SFA, CRM, and Sales Technologies (cont.)

Customer relationship management (CRM)
"CRM is a strategic approach that is concerned with creating improved shareholder value through the development of appropriate relationships with key customers and customer segments. CRM unites the potential of relationship marketing strategies and IT to create profitable, long-term relationships with customers and other key stakeholders. CRM provides enhanced opportunities to use data and information to both understand customers and cocreate value with them. This requires a cross-functional integration of processes, people, operations, and marketing capabilities that is enabled through information, technology, and applications."[18]
"CRM relates to strategy, the management of the dual creation of value, the intelligent use of data and technology, the acquisition of customer knowledge and the diffusion of this knowledge to the appropriate stakeholders, the development of appropriate (long-term) relationships with specific customers and/or customer groups, and the integration of processes across the many areas of the firm and across the network of firms that collaborate to generate customer value."[19]
Sales technology
"Sales technology refers to ITs that can facilitate or enable the performance of sales tasks."[2]

that SFA comprises a multitude of different IT and IS, which aim to increase sales force *efficiency and productivity* by either (a) automating some salesperson's activities and thereby increasing face-to-face selling time or (b) providing faster access to timely information.[21] According to SFA proponents, an increase in productivity is the outcome of freeing salespeople from administrative tasks, thus allowing them to spend more time in the field interacting with customers.[22] Accordingly, the basic characteristic of SFA is that it is intended to support routine (or repetitive) sales processes.[23]

Similar to the definitional problems related to SFA, it is also very difficult to come to an agreement as to what the conceptual boundaries of CRM are. Indeed, definitions vary widely across different stakeholder groups (e.g., vendors, consultants, and adopting firms), with each group giving its own definition.[24] In addition, there is no consensus among scholars on what should be an accepted conceptualization of CRM.[25] Notwithstanding this difficulty, in this book, we adopt Buttle's[26] CRM conceptualization, which has been set forth in the sales literature by Tanner and his colleagues.[27] According to Buttle's conceptualization, CRM comprises three different aspects: (a) strategic CRM, (b) analytical CRM, and (c) operational CRM.

Strategic CRM refers to the "managerial decision-making processes involved with defining and building a customer-oriented business strategy, business processes and culture, and requisite supporting technology models."[28] Analytical CRM refers to "the firm-level processes involved in analyzing customer and market-level information in order to provide the intelligence and insights that guide the firm's strategic marketing, CRM, service, and go-to-market choices."[29] Finally, operational CRM refers to "the specification of suitable and replicable business processes . . . designed to implement the firm's desired customer relationship model in terms of customer access, customer interaction, sales and channel choices, and customer learning at the one-on-one level."[30]

Based on this conceptualization, as well as the definitions presented in Table 1.1, three conclusions can be drawn. First, it is apparent that CRM technologies constitute just one aspect of CRM, which reflects a philosophy, a strategy, or an organizational process.[31] Though an important part of CRM, CRM technology itself is not identified with the enterprise-wide strategy and processes for managing customers at the strategic or analytical levels but rather is a subcomponent of CRM at the operational level.[32] As such, CRM technology is employed to help organizations realize intended CRM strategies and processes, which are designed at the strategic level and which aim at effectively and efficiently managing profitable customer relationships.[33]

Second, in contrast to SFA technologies, which facilitate routine activities, CRM technologies are targeted at helping salespeople develop customer knowledge and sales strategies that will facilitate the profitable management of customer relationships.[34] In other words, SFA is more operational and supports routine functions of a salesperson's job tasks, whereas CRM technology is more strategic by nature and aids in the development of selling and relationship strategies.[35]

Third, given the cross-functional and multichannel nature of CRM, CRM technology does not represent one thing. Rather, it encompasses a broad spectrum of technologies and applications that cover the entire gamut of customer-facing (or front-office) functions of a firm: marketing, service, and sales.[36] Echoing this sentiment, Srivastava, Shervani, and Fahey[37] argue that the development and execution of sales programs is only one subprocess in the overall CRM process of the organization. Put another way, CRM technology concerns a broader, enterprise-wide perspective of IS-IT, employed to automate and support all customer-facing aspects of a business.[38] For instance, marketing-based CRM technologies perform functions such as campaign, loyalty, segmentation, and list management; whereas service-based CRM technologies perform functions like call-center, customer self-service, and customer-care (help-desk) management. Given the intent of this book, our focus is on sales-based CRM technologies.[39] Specifically, sales-based CRM technologies refer to tools that are "specifically designed to help the sales organization meet its objectives in managing customer relationships."[40]

On the basis of the preceding discussion, it is apparent that SFA and sales-based CRM technology are different, but related, concepts. This view is consistent with Hunter and Perreault,[41] who drew a clear distinction between SFA and CRM systems as two distinct subsets or categories of sales technology. Hunter and Perreault's reasoning is that salespeople manage customer relationships by using a broader range of technology tools (e.g., mobile phones and spreadsheet-analysis software) than those typically falling within the realms of SFA or sales-based CRM technologies. Their logic has been adopted and extended by Rapp and his colleagues,[42] who also distinguish between SFA and CRM technology-use effects. We align with this line of research, and hence adopt the definition put forward by Hunter and Perreault,[43] according to which sales technology encompasses any "information technology that can facilitate or enable the performance of sales tasks such as sales-based CRM technologies and SFA technologies."

History and Evolution of Sales Technologies

Though using sales technologies may sound like a recent phenomenon, its dawn can be traced back to the late 1970s and early 1980s. During these early days of the revolution in office technology, firms have been using several devices to facilitate, automate, and streamline their selling processes. Thenceforward, however, sales technologies have evolved due to advances in information and communication technologies. Figure 1.1 graphically presents how sales technologies have evolved during the last 30 years, while Table 1.2 provides a detailed overview of these technologies.

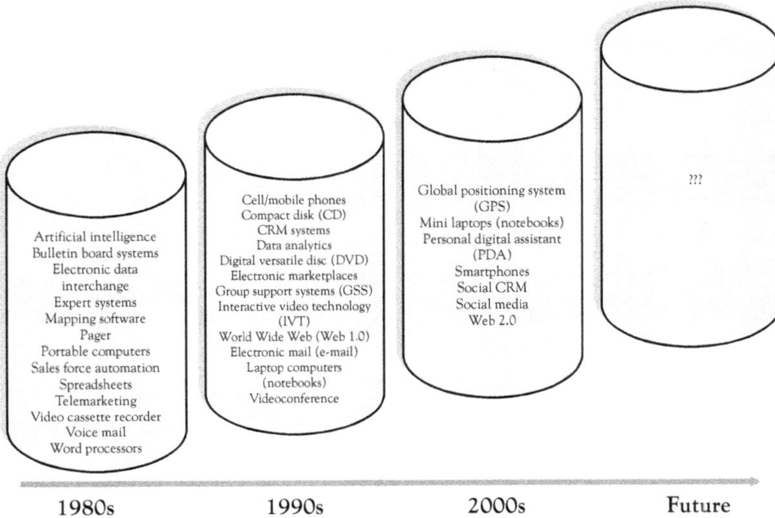

Figure 1.1. Evolution of sales technologies.

Note: Placing the various technologies in each chronological period was based on extant literature from the respective decade in which the technology experienced widespread adoption among sales organizations, rather than on the time the technology was invented.

The 1980s

The 1980s witnessed the advent of several revolutionary sales technologies. Perhaps the greatest revolution was the widespread availability of personal computers (or microcomputers) in organizational settings. Early proponents saw many advantages in using microcomputers for increasing the productivity of the sales function.[44] One important type of microcomputer that revolutionized the field of sales during the early 1980s was the portable computer.[45] Its introduction was the direct outcome of manufacturers' ability in developing personal devices that were small enough to be carried by salespeople during traveling and sales calls, though they "typically required power from an external source."[46] Portable computers were used by salespeople as a traveling companion to conduct spreadsheet analysis, process word documents, prepare bids, manage account information, manage contacts, develop sales reports, and send and receive electronic mails through dial-up telephony applications.[47] Some firms equipped their salespeople with pagers (or beepers) and voice mail systems that increased the availability and connectivity of their "road warriors" with customers and headquarters. Finally, a new technology—at the time—namely, the bulletin board system (BBS), spurred the connectivity of salespeople with the firm and increased intracompany information exchange. The BBS is a system of computers that allows users to connect with a firm's databases in order to read news and bulletins and exchange messages with each other.[48]

The introduction of computers and related technology changed not only the way salespeople were working but also how sales executives were managing their salespeople. For instance, the wide availability of microcomputers during the 1980s helped sales managers to analyze a vast amount of information in order to better assess sales potential, forecast sales, set sales budgets and goals, and design account strategies through the use of computerized applications such as spreadsheet analysis.[49] Also, the ample availability of videocassette recorders (VCRs) allowed sales management to modernize sales training activities and make learning more pleasant and effective for salespeople.

Other sales management applications involve the use of specialized mapping software that provides sales managers with an indispensable tool for visualizing, designing, and aligning sales territories;[50] the use of database management systems for tracking sales leads and prospects;[51] and the use of computer-based programs for efficiently allocating sales call time.[52]

An even more advanced form of computer usage for conducting sales management activities is what has been typically defined as an "expert system."[53] An expert system can be used by sales managers to solve problems and make optimal decisions by combining human experience with software and analytical and computing capabilities. Given the complexity of sales management decisions, there is a rich ground for applying expert systems in sales such as in compensation or motivation decisions.[54]

To help salespeople increase their productivity, firms began to experiment with artificial-intelligence technologies.[55] These technologies, combined with standard account management software, allow salespeople to generate account reports, organize their activities, manage accounts, analyze customer behavior, and forecast territory sales. More advanced intelligent systems can incorporate the knowledge of an "expert" into the system and can offer advices or suggest alternative courses of action during a sales encounter. Of course, artificial intelligence has also been applied to facilitating sales management activities such as sales forecasting.[56]

Another technology that was introduced during the 1980s is telemarketing, which refers to "a system staffed by trained specialists who utilize telecommunications and information technologies for the purpose of implementing marketing and sales programs in a cost effective way."[57] Telemarketing has been employed for a variety of sales activities, ranging from lead qualification, to order processing, to handling marginal accounts, and to providing customer service.[58]

Table 1.2. The Gamut of Sales Technologies

Sales technologies	Description
Cell/mobile phone	In general, a cell or mobile phone is a mobile telecommunications device that allows users to send and receive voice, text, audio, and video data.
Compact disk (CD)	An optical disk for recording and storing digital data that can be reproduced by a laser CD drive.
Data analytics software	Special software used to analyze and model raw data to aid in decision making.
Digital versatile disc (DVD)	A type of CD, but with a much larger storage capacity.
Electronic bulletin board system	A system of computers that allows users to connect with a company database in order to read news and bulletins and exchange messages with each other.[59]
Electronic data interchange (EDI)	"The movement of business data electronically between organizations in a structured, machine-retrievable data format that permits data to be transferred without rekeying from one computer program in one location to a computer program in another location."[60]
Electronic mail (e-mail)	In its simplest form, e-mail is a type of machine-mediated electronic communication of text messages.
Electronic marketplaces	An Internet-based platform for connecting buyers and sellers and facilitating sales exchanges.

Table 1.2. The Gamut of Sales Technologies (cont.)

Sales technologies	Description
Expert systems	"Computer-based software systems that interact with human decision makers to solve problems."[61]
Global positioning system (GPS)	A satellite-based navigation system that allows users to determine precise coordinates for anything located on the earth's surface.
Group support system (GSS)	"A GSS usually exists in a single room and consists of a group of networked personal computers (typically, about 20), sometimes with a large projection screen at the front of the room."[62] Today, GSS can take place in cyberspace.
Interactive video technology (IVT)	A combination of computer, laser disc, and video technologies that allow a user (i.e., a salesperson) to interact with the technology through a touch screen.
Laptop computer	The next generation of portable computers, which are truly portable machines since they weigh less than portables and are battery powered.[63]
Mapping software	Computer application that allows users to visualize, design, and align sales territories.
Mini laptop (or netbook)	A category of laptop computers that are very light and small compared to standard laptop computers, and that allow for easy wireless access to the Internet. Currently, they typically have a smaller processing capability than laptops.
Pager (or beeper)	A personal electronic device for receiving or sending short text messages. Contemporary devices are able to handle short message service (SMS) and e-mail messages.
Personal digital assistant (PDA)	A small, light, handheld electronic device that offers users many capabilities of a standard computer as well as Internet access or telephone capabilities.
Portable computer	"Personal computers that are designed to be carried long distances and that require access to an electrical outlet. They are essentially repackaged desktop machines with a smaller screen and a carrying handle; also called luggable or transportable computers."[64]

Table 1.2. The Gamut of Sales Technologies (cont.)

Sales technologies	Description
Smartphone	A type of mobile, computer-like phone that offers users more capabilities and applications than a standard mobile phone.
Social CRM	The next generation of CRM systems, which allow users to leverage the advantages of social networking and user-generated content to conduct essential sales activities.
Social media	New forms of media that are based on user participation and user-generated content, such as blogs, social networking sites, wikis, photo sharing, video sharing, and live casting.
Spreadsheet	A computer application that allows users to lay out and manage financial data entered into a table with rows and columns.[65]
Telemarketing	"A system staffed by trained specialists who utilize telecommunications and information technologies for the purpose of implementing marketing and sales programs in a effective way."[66]
Video cassette recorder (VCR)	A magnetic tape-recorder device for recording and reproducing videos.
Videoconference	A system of telecommunication technologies that allow a two-way exchange of video and audio data between two or more remotely located users.
Voice mail	A computerized telephone answering system that allows users to record, store, and retrieve telephone messages.
Web 2.0	The second generation of the Web that allows users to interact, interconnect, and network with each other as well as generate their own content.
Word processor	A computer application that allows users to manage (write, edit, and format) electronic documents.
World Wide Web (Web 1.0)	A global network of computers, hypertext documents, and other media.

The increased emphasis on interorganizational cooperation between trading partners in the same channel led to the development of the electronic data interchange (EDI). EDI refers to a cooperative interorganizational system comprising a set of telecommunication devices and computer applications that allow firms to electronically exchange information in a coded and structured format.[67] As such, EDI is not a sales technology used by individuals but rather refers to a technology utilized at the level of the firm. EDI has been adopted by many firms operating in such diverse industries as consumer packaged goods, chemicals, banking, automotives, and textiles.

The 1990s

Advances in computer science and applications during early 1990s made computers smaller, lighter, and energy independent. These portable computers were called laptop (or notebook) computers and were batter powered. As such, laptop computers forever changed the way salespeople were working since these machines gave salespeople the needed autonomy to use the laptop literally anywhere and at anytime. Advances in data recording and storage that appeared during the decade (i.e., CDs and DVDs) boosted the capabilities of laptop computers either for delivering multimedia sales presentations or for easier and quicker storage and retrieval of information.

The 1990s brought the evolution of the Internet as a new and powerful tool that changed the way firms conducted business forever. Electronic mail (e-mail) and the World Wide Web (or Web 1.0) are two of the most prominent Internet tools that had an immense impact on how selling is done.[68] The applications of Internet tools in sales are numerous, such as conducting sales training and meetings, and facilitating selling, payment, and order processing activities. In addition, in many industries, buyers and sellers started experimenting with electronic (or online) marketplaces that facilitate business exchanges and selling transactions.[69]

Because of the large amount of time salespeople spend traveling to call on customers, they experience a great loss of productive time. They also have to keep in constant touch with the firm headquarters, their supervisor, and their customers. It comes with little surprise, then, that sales organizations were eager to equip their sales forces with cell or mobile phone technology. The mobile phone was entered into sales organizations during late 1980s and early 1990s,[70] but it was not until late 1990s that the technology experienced a real acceleration in its adoption rate among sales organizations. Another telecommunication technology that was rapidly adopted during the 1990s is videoconferencing, which has been employed to conduct sales meetings and training and to facilitate team-based sales presentations to a group of buyers.

Old SFA technology was replaced by modern CRM systems during the 1990s. The evolution of mobile telephony, Internet services, and computer technology helped CRM systems become a powerful tool for field salespeople. These systems allowed salespeople to directly access product information, identify sales leads, and retrieve the latest customer information by using a wireless e-CRM application. Spawned by the overwhelming amount of information made available through CRM systems, many organizations started using data analytics software for mining terabytes of information and for improving decision-making processes.

The advent of microcomputers and video technologies during the 1990s led to many applications in sales management activities, including sales training. Essentially, microcomputers are used to facilitate the sales training process from initial salesperson assessment to knowledge development evaluation.[71] One such application involves the use of interactive video technology (IVT) in sales training.[72] IVT represents a combination of computer, laser disc, and video technologies that allows a user (i.e., a salesperson) to interact with the technology through a touch screen. The technology can be used to conduct role-plays and simulate sales calls. A second, somewhat simpler, application of technology in sales training is the self-paced video-enhanced training.[73] This type of training consists of videocassettes and written material delivered to salespeople, who then self-study the material in their spare time—no trainer is involved in the process of learning. Upon completion of the training session, the salesperson can call a toll-free number and take an exam.

Other applications of technology in sales management involve the utilization of Group Support Systems (GSS), which comprises a network of personal computers—either in the same physical space or in cyberspace—that is used to facilitate meetings, build consensus, stimulate brainstorming, and provide feedback in an environment that promotes candor and openness.[74]

The 2000s and Beyond

The dawn of the 21st century brought with it many new sales technologies in which firms have been investing in order to optimize their sales processes. One such evolution is the launch of mini laptops (or netbooks), which are very light and small compared to standard laptop computers and which allow for easy wireless access to the Internet. We have to note, however, that recent technological advances have blurred the traditional lines that used to distinguish telecommunication, telephony, and computer devices. As such, smartphones (i.e., a type of mobile, computer-like phone), mini laptops, and personal digital assistants are converging, with one device offering all of these capabilities (i.e., wireless Internet access, multimedia applications, word processors, spreadsheet analysis, and mobile phone services).

The nature and format of the Internet has evolved into Web 2.0, which refers to the second-generation of Web and which allows users to interact, interconnect, and network with each other as well as to generate their own content. Web 2.0 offers many new capabilities to sales organizations compared with its predecessor. One particularly relevant capability is the availability of social media. The term "social media" refers to new forms of media that are based on user participation and user-generated content, such as blogs, social networking sites, wikis, photo sharing, video sharing, live casting, and so forth. These media are changing the way salespeople work and, accordingly, how older CRM systems function. Specifically, contemporary CRM systems, which are increasingly being referred to as "social CRM," leverage the power of social networking and user-generated content to optimize the sales process. Given that customers are increasingly connected to each other through professional social networking sites and microblogging, firms need to engage in a continuing dialogue with these communities of customers. By so doing, salespeople may have more opportunities for expanding their own network of contacts, finding better sales leads, and increasing their productivity. Many modern sales-based CRM systems are now offering advanced modules to users, thereby promising to increase their effectiveness.

How will sales technologies evolve, and what will they look like in the near future? Though predicting the future of sales technologies is beyond the focus of this book, there are some trends that have already begun to emerge and will very likely impact sales technologies. One such trend is the advent of Web 3.0, which is conjectured to make the use of the Internet more personalized, interactive, and dynamic than its present form (Web 2.0). The content and structure of data will also be affected by this change, with more emphasis being placed on intelligent search engines that will analyze the semantic meaning of information. These advanced technologies will most likely have an immense impact on sales technologies, placing salespeople as central hubs in a huge network of leads and prospects, and on enhancing the capability of searching an ocean of relevant market information.

Types and Uses of Sales Technologies

At this point, one may ask whether sales technologies are used differently across firms or whether firms use different sales technologies. Though there are certain commonalities among firms, there is a considerable degree of variation in the usage of sales technologies across different selling contexts. In this book, we distinguish between two general classes of selling contexts, namely, the business-to-business (B2B) and the business-to-consumer (B2C) context. The two selling contexts differ with respect to how they define a "customer." Specifically, B2B firms target their selling efforts to other firms, organizations, and institutional customers who are not end users of the products they are selling; rather, these customers either use the product to produce their own goods and services, incorporate it into their own products, or simply resell it to others. In contrast, B2C firms sell directly to end user and consumer markets who buy to satisfy their own personal needs. Apparently, therefore, salespeople in each selling context are performing different sales activities. Though our focus in this book is on B2B selling contexts, for completeness, we will also make a separate reference to sales technologies utilized by B2C sales organizations.

Sales Technologies in the Business-to-Business Selling Context

As shown in Figure 1.2, sales technologies utilized by B2B firms can be distinguished into three groups, based on the type of activities they are supporting.[75] In particular, the three groups of technologies refer to sales technologies used for supporting (a) company-customer interface activities, (b) sales management activities, and (c) sales force activities. The usefulness of this classification lies in the fact that each of the three groups represents a different level in the sales hierarchy, namely, the organizational level, the sales management level, and the salesperson level, respectively. Table 1.3 lists some of the most prominent activities supported by each group of sales technologies. The list of activities is based on prior studies published in the literature, which provide detailed analyses regarding the various activities that are performed through the use of sales technologies.[76] We next discuss the technologies and their uses for each group.

Sales Technologies for Supporting Company-Customer Interface Activities

The first group of sales technologies refers to technologies used at the company-customer interface level, which involves interorganizational relationships between business partners in a marketing channel rather than relationships between individuals (e.g., a customer and a

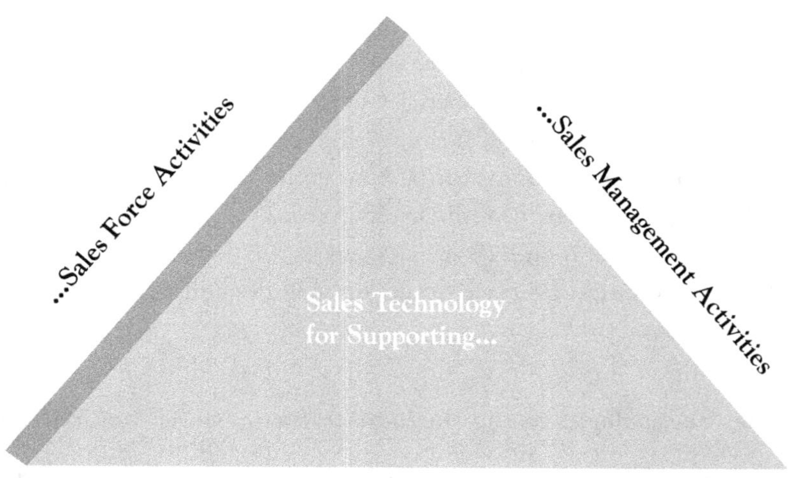

...Company-Customer Interface Activities

Figure 1.2. Types of sales technologies.

Table 1.3. Examples of Activities Supported by Sales Technologies

Company-customer interface activities	Sales management activities	Sales force activities
• Communication • Exchange documents • Information transfer/ exchange • Inventory management • Order management and processing • Process payment • Provide customer service	• Account management • Analyze customer information • Communicate with customers • Communicate with salespeople and headquarters • Cost and sales analysis • Design account strategies • Design sales compensation • Develop and deliver sales presentations • Evaluate sales force performance • Network with peers and customers • Sales force recruitment and selection • Sales force sizing and deployment • Sales force training • Sales forecasting • Sales process management • Seek customer information • Set goals and budgets • Spreadsheet analysis • Territory design • Word processing	• Account management • Analyze customer information • Check inventory • Check/configure prices • Communicate with customers • Communicate with headquarters and sales management • Contact management • Develop and deliver sales presentations • Expense reporting • Lead/prospect management • Network with peers and customers • Order management and processing • Prepare bids/proposals • Retrieve documentation/ product information • Sales call planning/ routing • Sales call reporting • Seek customer information • Spreadsheet analysis • Upload/download customer information • Word processing

salesperson). These technologies aim at automating the transactions of customers with their suppliers through the utilization of information and communication technologies. Thus, these technologies are not utilized by individual salespeople when conducting their job tasks but rather constitute interorganizational technologies that are employed at the organizational level. We next elaborate on two prominent examples of sales technologies at the company-customer interface.

One example of sales technology used at the company-customer interface is EDI. As previously mentioned, EDI is an electronic platform connecting buyers and sellers that uses a standardized application for exchanging information, processing orders, and issuing invoices.[77]

A second key technology falling into this category is the continuous replenishment program (CRP), which is an extension of EDI. The CRP possesses the following characteristics:[78] (a) buyers provide suppliers real-time information regarding their inventory levels and point-of-sales data, (b) the supplier is held responsible for replenishing buyers' inventories when these fall lower than a predetermined level, and (c) products are sold to retailers at an everyday low price. The CRP provides suppliers with the opportunity to provide better service by reducing customers' inventories and stockouts.

Both EDI and CRP are extensively applied across a wide range of industries, such as the consumer packaged goods (CPG) industry, where retailers are closely cooperating with CPG manufacturers.

Sales Technologies for Supporting Sales Management Activities

The second group of sales technologies is employed by sales managers across the sales hierarchy (e.g., field sales supervisors, district sales managers, chief sales executives, etc.) for effectively managing the sales force. These sales technologies help sales management perform essential managerial activities—such as setting sales budgets and goals, designing sales compensation packages, forecasting sales, and designing sales territories—in a more effective and efficient manner.[79] Specifically, sales managers utilize CRM technology to organize salespeople, evaluate alternative sales strategies, analyze account performance along the sales cycle, monitor the sales pipeline, and allocate sales resources in the most efficient manner. Moreover, CRM systems aid sales managers in tracking and monitoring sales force activities and results by providing a set of diagnostic metrics, thereby facilitating the process of performance evaluation. Finally, sales managers may use specialized mapping software, such as Geographic Information Systems (GIS), to design sales territories.[80]

In addition, they may use computerized programs to evaluate and select potential candidates and Internet-based multimedia software to train salespeople. Finally, they may use videoconferencing technologies to communicate with a team of buyers.[81]

We have to note, however, that the uses of sales technology across sales management levels may not be homogeneous; in fact, usage may considerably vary due to the different activities performed at each managerial level. As a general rule, the use of technology at the level of the field sales supervisor involves the performance of more tactical activities, whereas it gets more strategic as one moves to the upper echelons of sales management, such as the district, regional, divisional, and executive levels of management. For instance, frontline managers who are responsible for supervising field salespeople may use the technology mainly to monitor and evaluate individual salesperson performance and to communicate with their salespeople. Sales managers at higher levels may use technology for designing sales territories and for selecting new recruits, whereas chief sales executives may use sales technology to provide strategic direction, to assess the profitability of market segments, and to forecast business-unit sales.

Sales Technologies for Supporting Sales Force Activities

The third group of sales technologies refers to technologies used for supporting sales force activities. These technologies are utilized by individual salespeople and have created a new working reality by allowing salespeople to conduct many of their activities from a "virtual office." Recently, organizations have been equipping salespeople with a myriad of wireless technologies that allow them to instantly transmit voice, text, audio, and video data, thereby increasing their work performance, even from remote locations or while driving. We now discuss some examples of sales force technologies.

Nowadays, salespeople are using mobile phones and smartphones to organize their schedules and to be in constant touch with their customers and supervisors. In addition, they are using presentation software and multimedia devices to deliver sales presentations, netbooks to upload and download information about leads and accounts, e-mail to communicate with their peers and customers, and Web browsers to collect customer and competitive intelligence. They are also utilizing contact management software, inventory management systems, sales forecasting software, data analytics software, and global positioning systems.[82]

Sales technologies are employed by salespeople with a two-fold goal. On the one hand, technologies allow salespeople to conduct their activities more quickly and economically, thereby increasing their efficiency. On the other hand, technologies allow salespeople to know more about their customers and, consequently, to more effectively manage customer relationships.

Sales Technologies in the Business-to-Consumer Selling Context

While the primary thrust of this book focuses on sales technologies employed by B2B firms, as previoulsy mentioned, a reference is made here to sales technologies used by firms operating in the B2C domain. This is important since B2C selling reflects an important area of business activity and, subsequently, academic research. The discussion presented in this section draws primarily from the work of Ahearne and Rapp,[83] who have recently advanced a technology continuum to elaborate on the importance of the interaction between the customer and the salesperson, as well as the role of technology in this relationship. As the authors aptly note, while antecedents to technology acceptance in a B2C setting resemble those in a B2B setting, the salesperson-consumer interaction deserves special reference. This is so because in B2C settings, the technology that salespeople utilize is more visible to consumers, or the technology influences the interaction of consumers with the company and salespeople.

Consumers may use selling technologies in several ways. They can search for products, seek information, review products, interact with other consumers, manage their order process, and seek assistance and customer support. Ahearne and Rapp's technology continuum, referred to as the Salesperson-Customer Interface (SCI) Technology Continuum, includes five types of technologies. The first category is "salesperson-specific technologies." These technologies are built solely for the use of the salesperson, and the customer has no interaction with these technologies. Such technologies are used for conducting activities prior to and after a sales call. The second category is "salesperson-centric technologies," which refers to technologies employed by the salesperson in order to facilitate the sales transaction. These types of technologies may be visible to the customer. The third technology type is "salesperson-customer shared technologies," which are technologies that both the customer and the salesperson are actively engaged with throughout a sales interaction. The fourth type is labeled as "customer-centric technologies," which refers to technologies used by the customer to request and find information or to order a product. These technologies may or may not involve the salesperson. Finally, the fifth type of selling technologies is described as "customer-specific technologies," which are geared entirely toward the customer. The salesperson is not needed in this case, and customers use the technology through all stages of the sales process.

The Sales Technology Market

The world sales technology market is highly competitive, with some estimating that there are more than 600 vendors.[84] These vendors offer a wide range of SFA and sales-based CRM solutions—such as software-as-a-service applications and enterprise-wide CRM suites—to their customers. Though providing a full description of the entire industry is beyond the intent of this book, we provide a brief overview of the market. Specifically, according to a Gartner, Inc., study, [85] five of the world's biggest vendors—in terms of their market share—include such firms as SAP AG; Oracle; Salesforce.com, Inc.; Microsoft Corporation; and Amdocs. Of course, there are many other vendors that offer a multitude of sales technologies and applications, like Aplicor, Inc.; CDC Software; Cegedim; CRM ASP, Inc.; FrontRange Solutions USA, Inc.; Landslide Technologies, Inc.; Maximizer Software, Inc.; NetSuite, Inc.; RightNow Technologies, Inc.; Salesboom.com, Inc.; SalesNexus LLC; SalesPush Limited; SugarCRM, Inc.; and ZOHO Corp.[86]

Summary

As we saw in this chapter, the term "sales technology" is a rather broad term that encompasses such notions as SFA technologies and sales-based CRM systems. Sales technologies can be used differently depending on the nature of the job, the selling context, and the level in a firm's sales hierarchy where they are employed. Importantly, sales technologies have been hailed as an array of continually evolving technological tools that can transform the functioning of the sales organization. Consequently, sales technology vendors are offering a large number of different solutions to companies aiming at leveraging their selling capabilities.

CHAPTER 2

The Sales Technology Implementation Process

Chapter Overview

The aim of this chapter is to describe the sales technology implementation process. In particular, the chapter begins by defining the concept of implementation and delineating the various stages comprising the process. Attention is paid to elaborating on several notions that, though related, differ from implementation to a significant degree. Next, we present, in detail, a series of models that pertain to technology acceptance at the individual level. Collectively, these models provide a comprehensive picture of the theoretical rationale underlying end-user technology acceptance.

The Implementation Process

Defining Implementation

Undoubtedly, sales technologies can help sales organizations boost productivity and come closer to meeting customer needs. Business reality, however, reveals that there is much left to be desired in initial planning. As evidenced in a plethora of studies that have been conducted over the last 15 years, most sales technologies fail to be successfully implemented, largely due to ineffective management processes as well as high levels of sales force resistance.[1] As such, scrutinizing the implementation process should provide managers with a hands-on tool to successfully roll out technological innovations in the sales organization. Before we proceed in discussing the implementation process, it is important to first focus on defining the notion of implementation itself. This is critical for the study of technology acceptance within organizations, since the concept of implementation is often confused with other related, though different, concepts, such as adoption or acceptance of IT. Let us first begin by defining the concept of adoption.

Though several definitions of organizational-level adoption exist in the extant literature, two appear to be the most widely accepted within the scholarly community. The first definition refers to adoption of an innovation as "an organization's decision to install an innovation within the organization."[2] The second definition is owed to E. Rogers,[3] who views adoption as "the decision to make full use of an innovation as the best course of action available." Though somewhat different, the two definitions share two common themes: (a) adoption involves a deliberate decision and (b) adoption of an innovation precedes its use.

On the other hand, implementation of an innovation, such as SFA or a sales-based CRM system, refers to "the transition period during which targeted organizational members ideally become increasingly skillful, consistent, and committed in their use of an innovation."[4] Other researchers take a technological-diffusion perspective, where IT implementation is defined as "an organizational effort directed toward diffusing appropriate information technology within a user community."[5]

In the case of sales technology, targeted employees who are expected to use or support it are salespeople and managerial employees across the entire sales hierarchy (e.g., field sales supervisors, district sales managers, sales executives, etc.).

On the basis of the aforementioned definitions of implementation, one can draw four conclusions:

1. Implementation takes considerable time to complete; thus, it can be approached as a planned process rather as a one-time event.
2. It is apparent that adoption precedes implementation since an innovation's committed use should logically follow the organization's decision to adopt it.
3. Implementation involves gradually increasing levels of innovation use.
4. Successfully implementing an innovation entails that individual users must decide to adopt the innovation following the organization's decision to adopt it.

Supportive evidence for these conclusions comes from the work of Frambach and Schillewaert,[6] who, based on prior research, argue that adoption mediates the initiation and implementation stages in the adoption process. As they note, "This organizational adoption decision is only the beginning of implementation. The acceptance or assimilation within the organization now becomes important." We now turn our attention to elaborating on the various stages of the implementation process.

Stages in the Implementation Process

Implementing innovations and technologies within consumer and professional employee communities has long occupied the minds of researchers in a wide range of scientific domains. Specifically, theoretical perspectives have been advanced based on such diverse lines of inquiry as sales technology, technology diffusion, innovation adoption, organizational change, and information technology.[7] Table 2.1 presents a summary of five major perspectives and models that have appeared in the literature that relate to the process of implementation at the level of the individual user. In what follows, we briefly discuss each one.

Cooper and Zmud[8] take a technology diffusion perspective to propose a six-stage model of IT implementation. During the initiation stage, firms become aware of their need to purchase an information technology, start searching for solutions, evaluate potential vendors and systems, and make the decision to buy. During the second stage (adoption), the organization invests resources and buys a system, and during the third stage (adaptation), the system is developed, installed, and maintained, and users are provided with training. The next stage, that is, the acceptance stage, involves the formal introduction of the system into organizational life, and users are induced to start using it. During the routinization stage, users are encouraged to use the system, which is viewed as a component of organizational reality. Finally, during the final stage (infusion), the system is used to its fullest potential.

The second perspective concerns the diffusion of innovations within consumer populations.[9] Despite the differing context, this perspective offers a comprehensive conceptualization that can aid overall understanding of how technologies are successfully implemented. Specifically, this perspective goes beyond adoption to studying a technology's use after

Table 2.1. *Summary of Perspectives on Implementation Process*
Perspective

Technology diffusion (Cooper & Zmud, 1990)	Use-diffusion (Shih & Venkatesh, 2004)	Planned organizational change (Lewin, 1952)	Innovation implementation (Klein & Sorra, 1996)	Sales technology implementation (Sundaram, Schwarz, Jones, & Chin, 2007)
• Initiation • Adoption • Adaptation • Acceptance • Routinization • Infusion	• Adoption • Use (variety and rate) • Diffusion	• Unfreezing • Moving • Refreezing	• Adoption • Implementation	• Predeployment attitude and intention • Frequency • Routinization • Infusion

consumers have adopted it. Thus, the focus of the model is on postadoption usage behaviors. The authors conceptualize usage as a two dimensional construct. The first dimension refers to variety of use (i.e., the different ways the technology is used), while the second refers to rate of use (i.e., the time an individual spends using the product during a certain period). According to the model, effective diffusion results when users make intense use of a technology (i.e., they exhibit high levels on both variety and rate of use).

Lewin's[10] model of planned organizational change was not specifically developed for studying technology implementation, but it has been frequently employed in technology implementation research.[11] Given that technology changes or radically alters current work practices, the model offers a useful lens for examining change processes associated with technology implementation. The model consists of three stages: (a) an unfreezing stage, where users are freeing themselves from the patterns of behavior in existence prior to the introduction of change; (b) a moving stage, during which users gather new information and learn new behaviors that can help improve their performance; and (c) a refreezing stage, where users make the new behaviors an integral part of their work routines.

The fourth model presents a two-stage innovation implementation process.[12] The model takes the perspective of the user and thus falls within the realm of user-based stage models.[13] During the first stage, namely, the adoption stage, the organization decides to adopt a specific technology that is then introduced to users. It is at this stage (i.e., the implementation stage) where users employ the system for a prolonged period of time until they become skilled, enthusiastic, and consistent users of the system.

Finally, the fifth and most recent model was introduced by Sundaram, Schwarz, Jones, and Chin,[14] and deals with implementation in the specific context of sales technology. The authors synthesize past research from sales and IT literature and present a process model of sales technology implementation that comprises four distinct stages. The first stage refers to an individual's predeployment attitude toward technology and her or his intentions to use it before receiving it. These attitudes and intentions are hypothesized to directly influence actual usage after system deployment. However, usage is not conceptualized as one thing but rather comprises three different types, namely frequency, routinization, and infusion, all of which are temporally distinct. Specifically, at the time when the system is introduced to the organization, users start using it to a great extent or with great frequency (stage two). Next, users incorporate it into their routine work patterns (stage three) until they fully use the system to enhance productivity (stage four).

Despite the differences in constructs and theoretical approaches that each perspective has employed in order to study implementation, one common theme that cuts across the models is that implementation can be conceptualized as a *process* with specific and distinguishable stages.[15]

A second common theme is that the stages proposed by each perspective are closely related. For instance, the initiation stage in the technology diffusion perspective is related to (a) the unfreezing stage in the organizational change model, (b) the adoption stage in the innovation implementation model, and (c) the predeployment attitude or intention stage in the sales technology implementation model.

Drawing on and synthesizing the aforementioned perspectives, we develop a generic model of the sales technology implementation process that is displayed in Figure 2.1. Similar to user-based stage models of innovation process that focus on the perspective of the user, our conceptualization aims at delineating the stages through which a sales technology evolves until users fully integrate it into their behavioral repertoire.[16] As shown in Figure 2.1, the implementation process involves a series of stages that occur over time and in a sequential fashion. In other words, moving to the next stage presupposes the effective completion of the preceding one, as each stage is temporally distinct.

According to the model presented in Figure 2.1, there are three generic stages characterizing the entire process of technology implementation:[17] (a) the preadoption stage, which involves activities such as awareness of the need to buy a technology, seeking and evaluating potential vendors, and making the decision to buy the IT; (b) the adoption stage, where both the organization and individual users decide to adopt and use the technology; and (c) the postadoption stage, which involves behaviors that users engage in toward making the technology an integral part of their work routines after the technology has been introduced to them.

Several implications can be drawn from the proposed model. First, the adoption of an innovation, such as a sales-based CRM system, is a

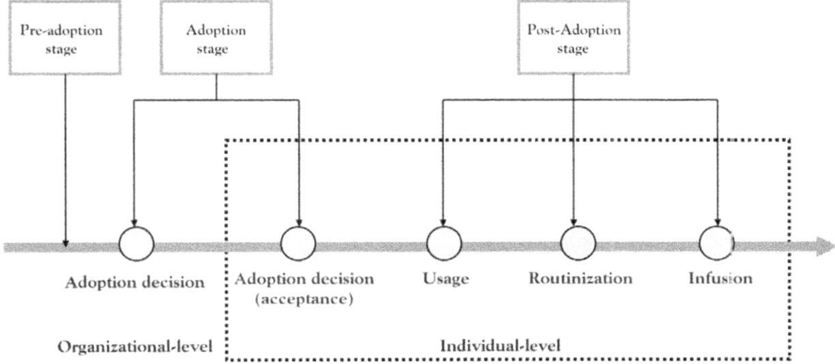

Figure 2.1. A generic model of the sales technology implementation process.

decision made at both the organizational and individual levels.[18] Specifically, at the inaugural stage of the process, the organization decides to adopt and install an innovation. This decision is driven by several factors, such the organization's strategy, its objectives, and the situation it confronts in its market.[19] After the organization has decided to buy and install the innovation, individual employees are called on to adopt the innovation and start using it. Thus, innovation also takes place at the individual level, but only after the organization has adopted it—this phenomenon has been described as "dual-adoption."[20] Adoption at the individual level is usually termed "acceptance," which refers to the decision of individuals to either adopt or reject an innovation in their work activities. This distinction between adoption at the organizational level and acceptance at the individual level is important because it helps us understand the nature of implementation, which involves decisions made by both the organization and the individuals who are going to use the technology. Moreover, it is important to note that an individual's decision to adopt (accept) the technology follows that of the organization, and thus there is a temporal distance between the two decisions. Though implementation is planned at higher levels of the organization, it can only be successful if individual salespeople accept it and start using it.

Second, once individuals have decided to accept the technology, they start experimenting with it—it is at this stage at which actual usage begins to take place. As Klein and Sorra[21] argue, however, use of an innovation does not simply involve one action—it can range from non-use (i.e., avoiding use) of the innovation, to compliance, to committed use. Initially, users experiment and test the usefulness of the new technology until they progressively start using the system to a great extent. It is only after this stage that users are making the system part of their routine and, hopefully, are making optimal use of it in order to infuse the system into their behavioral repertoire.[22]

To achieve implementation effectiveness, therefore, the technology has to be consistently and enthusiastically used by individuals. Thus, the duration and the frequency of technology usage is a necessary, though not sufficient, condition for implementation effectiveness, which refers to "the consistency and quality of targeted organizational members' use of a specific innovation."[23] As users make more intensive and extensive use of a given technology, the latter is increasingly embedded within an organization's governance system (i.e., routinization) and eventually within the operational and managerial work systems (i.e., infusion).[24] Consequently, this logic suggests that it is the extended use of a sales technology that leads to technology routinization, which, in turn, leads to technology infusion.[25] That said, however, it is now time to sound a note of caution regarding usage. Usage should be optimally, not maximally, increased among members of the sales force by carefully allocating time spent across different activities. According to one study,[26] salesperson usage and performance are not linearly related; rather, there is an inverted u-shaped relationship between the two variables. In other words, usage exerts a positive effect on sales performance to a specific point—beyond that point, usage has diminishing returns and actually lowers performance. One explanation for this nonlinear relationship is that salespeople are primarily concerned with building and maintaining customer relationships, through which they achieve sales results. Given that the time that salespeople have is a scarce resource, a higher degree of usage may mean that salespeople are using field time—during which they normally call on customers—to use a new technology, thus hurting their performance.

Third, the aforementioned discussion leads us to the realization that the effective incorporation of a sales technology into the sales force's current work practices can only be accomplished if a critical mass of salespeople uses the technology to its fullest capacity. It is important to note, however, that it is not uncommon to observe some salespeople using the technology to a great extent and others using it less frequently, even within the same organization.[27]

A final implication of the proposed process is that implementation can be approached as a planned process, in the sense that executives can manage the entire process by carefully planning, analyzing, and monitoring the effective completion of each stage.

Models of Technology Acceptance

As discussed previously, one stage in the implementation process is concerned with adoption and acceptance of technology by individual users. Given the stage's importance for effectively diffusing a planned technological initiative in a user population, a lot of ink has been spilled on investigating the antecedents (or predictors) of IT acceptance during the past 30 years. Many of these research efforts have adapted and extended theoretical frameworks originally developed for explaining social and psychological behavior to the specific area of technology acceptance. These comprehensive models have been subjected to extensive empirical testing, and they therefore offer managing practitioners quite robust conclusions pertaining to why and whether employees accept and use technological innovations such as sales technology. Our aims are to illuminate the mechanisms that underlie effective sales technology implementation and to shed light on a fundamental question: why, and under what conditions, will users adopt or accept an IT? Accordingly, this section presents a detailed overview of the most prominent technology acceptance models that have been offered in the scientific literature.[28]

Theory of Reasoned Action (TRA)

The Theory of Reasoned Action (TRA) was introduced into the social-psychological literature by Ajzen and Fishbein in order to explain the reasons that make people engage in consciously intended behaviors.[29] Since then, TRA has been particularly successful in predicting and explaining behaviors across a wide variety of domains. As such, it is not surprising that researchers have applied TRA to the context of IT usage, a special case of behavior in a work setting.[30] We now proceed in describing this theoretical framework, the core elements of which are presented in Table 2.2.

According to TRA, an employee's actual behaviors are influenced by behavioral intentions, which, in turn, are influenced by attitudes toward the behavior and subjective norm. Behavioral intention refers to the strength or probability of one's intention to perform a behavior,[31] whereas attitude refers to one's positive or negative feelings (evaluative affect) about performing the target behavior.[32] Subjective norms involve one's perceptions that most people considered important to him or her think that he or she should or should not perform the behavior in question.[33]

The model also postulates that attitude is an outcome of beliefs and evaluations, which represent one's judgments about the importance of consequences of the specific behavior. For instance, a salesperson may form a positive attitude toward using sales technology when he or she thinks that using it will result in a favorable outcome, such as increasing productivity. Subjective norms are an outcome of normative beliefs and motivation to comply, which represent what an individual thinks important others expect him or her to do regarding a specific behavior (e.g., using IT), as well as his or her motivation to comply with these expectations.

One implication of this theory is that attitudes and subjective norms mediate[34] the effects of other variables on intentions, and that intentions mediate the impact of attitudes and subjective norms on behavior.[35] Thus, in order to understand how organizational or other environmental characteristics influence IT usage (i.e., a specific behavior), researchers need to consider and study the mediating role of attitudes, subjective norms, and behavioral intentions. However, one early empirical study[36] provides mixed support for this supposition. Specifically, the study shows

Table 2.2. The Theory of Reasoned Action (TRA)

Predictors	Mediators	Moderators	Outcome(s)
• Beliefs and evaluations	• Attitudes toward behavior	• Experience	• Actual behavior
• Normative beliefs and motivation to comply	• Subjective norms • Behavioral intentions		

that while behavioral intentions is indeed an important predictor of technology usage, attitudes and subjective norms play a lesser role in mediating the effects of beliefs on intentions—at least to a lesser extent than predicted by TRA.

Though the original model, as offered by Fishbein and Ajzen, does not predict any boundary conditions, several researchers extended this framework by adding moderators[37] to the frameworks relationships. For example, one study found that attitudes play a more important role with increasing levels of experience, while the opposite was found for subjective norms.[38]

Technology Acceptance Model (TAM)

In spite of the richness and soundness of TRA, the model represents a general conceptualization of human behavior. Put another way, the model was not specifically designed to explain why employees accept or reject information technologies. Spawned by this reality, Davis[39] extended TRA to the domain of technological acceptance by developing the technology acceptance model (TAM). TAM is an important addition to the literature since it provides a parsimonious explanation of end-user technology acceptance that can be applied to a wide variety of contexts.

TAM uses the core tenets of TRA to provide a simpler explanation of technology acceptance (see Table 2.3). In particular, similar to TRA, TAM posits that actual system use is influenced by a behavioral intention to use it. However, there are some important differences between the two frameworks.

Table 2.3. Technology Acceptance Model (TAM)

Predictors	Mediators	Moderators	Outcome(s)
• Perceived ease of use • Perceived usefulness • External variables	• Intention to use	• Experience • Gender • Usage type	• Usage behavior

First, unlike TRA, TAM posits no influence of subjective norms on usage behavior and therefore does not include the construct of subjective norms in the model.

Second, TAM introduces two particular beliefs, namely, perceived usefulness and perceived ease of use, that jointly affect an individual's actual system usage through their effects on behavioral intention to use technology. Perceived usefulness refers to "the degree to which an individual believes that using a particular system will enhance his/her job performance,"[40] while perceived ease of use is defined as "the degree to which an individual believes that using a particular system would be free of effort."[41] According to TAM, perceived ease of use is theorized as a causal antecedent of perceived usefulness.

Third, whereas TRA postulates that attitude toward the technology completely mediates the effect of beliefs, such as perceived usefulness, on behavioral intentions, TAM allows for a direct effect of usefulness on intentions. As noted by Davis, Bagozzi, and Warshaw,[42] the direct link between usefulness and behavioral intention could be explained by the logic that employees may "form intentions toward behaviors they believe will increase their job performance, over and above whatever positive or negative feelings may be evoked toward the behavior per se."

Finally, TAM acknowledges that usefulness and ease of use may be influenced by a set of external variables, like organizational support, training, system characteristics, and so forth.

Though usefulness and ease of use are both important for explaining intentions to use a technology, usefulness has consistently been found to outperform ease of use in terms of its effects on behavioral intentions. One study,[43] for instance, found that the effect of ease of use on behavioral intention declines over time as users gain experience in using the system; in contrast, the effect of usefulness on intention was strong even after a significant period of time. A second study[44] provides evidence that gender plays an important role in explaining the effects of usefulness and ease of use; specifically, the study shows that usefulness is more salient for men, while ease of use is more salient for women.

Since its introduction to the literature, TAM has been widely employed in various studies predicting the use of almost any kind of technology and innovation, such as the use of World Wide Web, e-mail, SFA, and CRM systems.[45] The vast number of studies employing TAM has been successfully summarized into two recent meta-analytic works.[46] In other instances, the original TAM has been extended or modified to provide a more comprehensive picture of technology acceptance and to fit different contexts.[47] Despite its usefulness, however, it should be noted that several researchers have raised concerns regarding the validity of TAM;[48] nevertheless, the evidence from previous studies suggests that TAM is a valid model that can be employed to predict and explain technology acceptance.

Technology Acceptance Model 2 (TAM2)

As stated previously, TAM offers a parsimonious and valid theoretical framework for predicting and explaining end-user technology acceptance. However, some researchers went further, extending the framework by refining its core constructs. In particular, Venkatesh and Davis[49] introduced an extended form of TAM, which is thenceforth called TAM2. Drawing on TAM, TAM2 conceptualizes perceived usefulness as an important construct that influences usage behavior through intentions to use. Also, TAM2 incorporates two additional sets of theoretical constructs that function as antecedents to perceived usefulness (see Table 2.4).

The first set of antecedents comprises (a) subjective norm, (b) voluntariness, and (c) image, which are collectively labeled as "social influence processes." The idea of subjective norm draws on the same notion

Table 2.4. Extension of the Technology Acceptance Model (TAM2)

Predictors	Mediators	Moderators	Outcome(s)
Social influence processes • Subjective norm • Voluntariness • Image *Cognitive instrumental processes* • Job relevance • Output quality • Result demonstrability • Perceived ease of use	• Perceived usefulness • Intention to use	• Experience • Voluntariness	Usage behavior

employed in TRA. However, TAM2 posits a direct impact of subjective norms on intention to use. This supposition is supported by a recent meta-analysis conducted in the domain of information technology research.[50] Voluntariness is defined as "the extent to which potential adopters perceive the adoption decision to be non-mandatory."[51] In TAM2, voluntariness is hypothesized to exert a moderating effect on the relationship between subjective norm and intention to use, such that subjective norm will have a positive direct effect on intention to use only when system use is perceived to be mandatory. In addition, subjective norms are expected to have a positive direct effect on perceived usefulness.

According to TAM2, the positive direct effect of subjective norms on intentions for mandatory usage contexts will weaken over time as users gain experience. Finally, the model predicts a moderating effect of experience on the positive relationship between subjective norms and perceived usefulness, such that in both mandatory and voluntary contexts, the relationships will weaken as users gain experience.

The second set of antecedents, which is expected to exert a positive direct influence on perceived usefulness, is labeled "cognitive instrumental processes." This set of antecedents consists of (a) job relevance, (b) output quality, (c) result demonstrability, and (d) perceived ease of use. Job relevance refers to how applicable the technology is perceived to one's job. Output quality concerns the degree to which a technology can perform job tasks in a good manner. Result demonstrability refers to "the tangibility of the results of using the innovation."[52] Finally, perceived ease of use has the same meaning as in the TAM.

Motivational Model (MM)

Psychological-motivation theories have been extensively employed to study human behavior in work settings. Given the robustness and importance of these theories, some researchers have adapted them to a technology acceptance context. The work of Davis, Bagozzi, and Warshaw[53] represents such an early effort. Specifically, the authors developed the motivational model (MM), which complements the TAM by incorporating enjoyment—besides perceived usefulness—as an antecedent of intention to use a technology. Enjoyment refers to "the extent to which the activity of using the computer is perceived to be enjoyable in its own right, apart from any performance consequences that may be anticipated."[54] The components of this model are presented in Table 2.5. According to MM, output quality and perceived ease of use impact perceived usefulness and enjoyment, which, in turn, are related to intentions to use a system. Further, the model posits that intentions to use mediate the influence of perceived usefulness and enjoyment on system usage. Finally, MM assumes that task importance will moderate the relationships between ease of use and output quality with perceived usefulness.

MM is rooted in motivation theories,[55] where motivation can take one of two forms: extrinsic motivation and intrinsic motivation. Extrinsic motivation refers to "the performance of an activity because it is perceived to be instrumental in achieving valued outcomes that are distinct from the activity itself, such as improved job performance, pay, or promotions,"[56] whereas intrinsic motivation is defined as "the performance of an activity for no apparent reinforcement other than the process of performing the activity per se."[57] From a motivational perspective, therefore, perceived usefulness can be considered as a form of extrinsic motivation, while enjoyment is a form of intrinsic motivation.

Several interesting findings emerged in the first empirical test of MM.[58] First, consistent with TRA and TAM, intention to use is strongly related to usage behavior. Second, users' intentions to use a technology will be influenced not only by its perceived usefulness but also by more intrinsic aspects of motivation, such as the degree of enjoyment that users receive by using the system. Though usefulness is more strongly related to intentions than enjoyment, the latter continues to exert an influence on intentions even when the degree of usefulness stays the same. As such, an important implication of MM is that information systems should primarily be useful but nevertheless allow users to derive a sense of enjoyment

Table 2.5. Motivational Model of Technology Use (MM)

Predictors	Mediators	Moderators	Outcome(s)
• Output quality • Perceived ease of use	• Perceived usefulness • Enjoyment • Intentions to use	• Task importance	• System usage

from using them. However, doing so implies that the system is easy to use and capable of producing high-quality output.

Theory of Planned Behavior (TPB)

The theory of planned behavior (TPB), which was originally introduced by Ajzen,[59] is basically an extension of TRA. The basic difference between TRA and TPB theories is that TPB introduces perceived behavioral control as a new construct. TPB has received significant research attention and empirical support in its ability to predict behavior in a variety of work settings.[60]

TPB differs from TAM to a significant extent. According to Mathieson,[61] the two theories differ in three respects. First, TAM uses beliefs that can be employed regardless of the implementation context. However, TPB posits that beliefs are specific to the context under investigation, thus making the theory more specific. Second, TAM does not explicitly include any social variables, whereas TPB does. Third, TPB introduces a new construct, namely, perceived behavioral control, which is defined as "the perceptions of internal and external constraints on behavior."[62]

In general, TPB appears to be a rich theoretical framework that can be used by practitioners to examine system usage. In spite of this general recognition, the empirical evidence points out some of the theory's limitations. Specifically, Mathieson[63] applied the theory in the context of technology acceptance and contrasted its explanatory power with TAM. The author found that both TAM and TPB predicted intention to use an IT quite well, with TAM having a slight empirical advantage. However, when the goal is to study, in detail, why users may or may not be satisfied with a technology, TPB appears more relevant than TAM.[64]

Table 2.6 lists the main elements of TPB. According to the model, usage behavior is a function of intentions, which are jointly determined by three factors: (a) attitude, (b) subjective norm, and (c) perceived behavioral control. Each of these factors is in turn influenced by different facets of beliefs.

Attitude is predicted by behavioral beliefs and outcome evaluations. A behavioral belief is "the subjective probability that the behavior will lead to a particular outcome"[65]—such as, using a system will free time from administrative work or improve ability to support a sales presentation.

Table 2.6. The Theory of Planned Behavior (TPB)

Predictors	Mediators	Moderators	Outcome(s)
• Behavioral beliefs and outcome evaluations • Normative beliefs and motivation to comply • Control beliefs and perceived facilitation	• Attitude • Subjective norm • Perceived behavioral control	• Gender • Experience	• Usage behavior • Intention to use

Outcome evaluation is "a rating of the desirability of the outcome"[66]—such as, how desirable is it for salespeople to have real-time access to order processing and pricing data by using a particular sales technology.

The variable of subjective norm is hypothesized to be influenced by normative beliefs and motivation to comply. A normative belief refers to an "individual's perception of a referent other's opinion about the individual's performance of the behavior."[67] In sales organizations, salespeople often view the opinions of peers, customers, and especially sales managers as very important influences in the formation of their belief structures. This is because sales managers are often regarded as trusted mentors or, in the absence of a trusted relationship with the salesperson, as simply being able to enact reward and punishment mechanisms. Motivation to comply is "the extent to which the person wants to comply with the wishes of the referent other."[68] A salesperson, for instance, may choose to comply with the demands of her customers but not with what peers are saying, since she may regard the opinion of customers as more important than her peers.

Perceived behavioral control is a function of control beliefs and perceived facilitation. Control beliefs are the "perception of the availability of skills, resources, and opportunities," whereas perceived facilitation is "the individual's assessment of the importance of those resources to the achievement of outcomes."[69] For instance, a salesperson may view the provision of system training and technical support (i.e., control beliefs) as being very important for her to make effective use of a sales technology (i.e., perceived facilitation).

We should note that some of the relationships between constructs in TPB may be moderated by the demographic characteristics of users. For instance, it has been found that (a) gender and experience may moderate the impact of attitudes on intentions, such as that the relationship is stronger for men and for younger employees, and (b) subjective norm and perceived behavioral control have a stronger influence on intentions for less-experienced women.[70]

Combined TAM and TPB (TAM-TPB)

Given the preponderance of TAM in technology acceptance research and the theoretical richness of TPB, it was natural for some researchers to consider combining the two theories into an integrated framework. The rationale is that, unlike TPB, TAM does not include social and control factors as predictors of behavior. Accordingly, Taylor and Todd[71] were the first to combine TAM with TPB in what they termed the "augmented TAM." The elements of the combined TAM-TPB conceptualization are shown in Table 2.7.

According to the combined TAM-TPB model, behavior (i.e., system usage) is influenced by behavioral intention, which, in turn, is influenced by attitude, subjective norm, perceived behavioral control, and perceived usefulness. Attitude, subjective norm, and perceived behavioral control are TPB-TRA constructs, whereas perceived usefulness originates from TAM conceptualization.

The combined TAM-TPB also predicts that perceived behavioral control will have a direct effect on behavior in addition to its indirect effect through intentions. Perceived usefulness and perceived ease of use are determinants of attitude, whereas perceived ease of use directly affects perceived usefulness.

Table 2.7. The Combined TAM and TPB (C-TAM-TPB)

Predictors	Mediators	Moderators	Outcome(s)
• Perceived usefulness • Perceived ease of use	• Attitude • Subjective norm • Perceived behavioral control • Intention to use	• Experience	• Usage behavior

Taylor and Todd[72] posited that the relationships among the constructs appearing in the combined TAM-TPB model would be moderated by user experience. Their empirical study substantiated this assumption since the impact of perceived usefulness, attitude, and perceived behavioral control on behavioral intentions was stronger in the case of users with relatively more experience. In contrast, the impact of subjective norm was attenuated under high levels of experience. An apparent implication of Taylor and Todd's study is that when firms design and implement an IT, they should take into account the level of the user's experience, since less experienced users will tend to rely on different factors (e.g., perceived usefulness) than experienced ones in order to start using the system.

Model of PC Utilization (MPCU)

A rather competing perspective to those presented by TRA and TPB is offered by the model of PC utilization (MPCU). MPCU was introduced by Thompson, Higgins, and Howell[73] and draws directly from the theory of interpersonal behavior.[74] The model was an early effort to predict PC utilization in work settings and focused at usage behavior rather than intention to use.[75] Table 2.8 lists the constructs employed in this model.

As seen in Table 2.8, MPCU posits that six predictors exert a direct influence on the degree of PC utilization. All six predictors correspond to the categories of behavioral influences described in the theory of interpersonal behavior.[76] The first three factors fall under an umbrella term, namely, "perceived consequences," whereas the last three factors correspond to the categories "affect," "social factors," and "facilitating conditions," respectively. More analytically, the first predictor displayed in

Table 2.8. The Model of PC Utilization (MPCU)

Predictors	Moderators	Outcome(s)
• Long-term consequences of PC use	• Experience	• Utilization of PC
• Job fit with PC use		
• Complexity of PC use		
• Affect toward PC use		
• Social factors influencing PC use		
• Facilitating conditions of PC use		

Table 2.8 refers to the long-term consequences of PC use or "the out-comes that have a pay-off in the future."[77]

The second predictor is related to job fit with PC use, which refers to the "extent to which an individual believes that using a PC can enhance the performance of his or her job."[78] For example, a salesperson may view sales technology as particularly helpful in facilitating access to customer data and, accordingly, planning individual selling strategies. Apparently, job fit is a similar conceptualization to TAM's "perceived usefulness."

The third predictor is complexity of PC use, which is defined as "the degree to which an innovation is perceived as relatively difficult to under-stand and use."[79] Complexity can therefore be viewed as the opposite of perceived ease of use, which is included in TAM. Accordingly, the model predicts that complexity will be negatively related to technology usage.

The fourth predictor is termed "affect toward PC use" and is defined as "the feelings of joy, elation, or pleasure, or depression, dis-gust, displeasure, or hate associated by an individual with a particu-lar act."[80] It therefore represents an affective attitude of salespeople toward using a particular technology.

The fifth predictor relates to the social factors influencing PC use, and they refer to an "individual's internalization of the reference groups' subjective culture, and specific interpersonal agreements that the indi-vidual has made with others, in specific social situations."[81] Thompson, Higgins, and Howell[82] specifically refer to roles, norms, and values that collectively compose subjective culture in an organizational context.

Finally, the sixth predictor refers to facilitating conditions of PC use, which are defined as "objective factors, 'out there' in the environment, that several judges or observers can agree make an act easy to do."[83] Such facilitating conditions may include, inter alia, the provision of training and technical support to salespeople who are called on to use a sales technology.

In their empirical study, Thompson, Higgins, and Howell[84] found that social factors, complexity, job fit, and long-term consequences had significant effects on PC utilization; however, they did not find support for the hypothesized impact of affect and facilitating conditions on tech-nology usage. In addition, consistent with TAM's predictions, they found that job fit, a notion that resembles perceived usefulness in TAM's termi-nology, has a larger impact on usage as compared to complexity, which is similar to perceived ease of use included in the TAM conceptualization.

Another study[85] tested the moderating influences of user experience (as measured by self-reported skill level and length of time having used personal computers) on the MPCU's construct interrelationships. The results highlight that whereas the impact of complexity affect, social factors, and facilitating conditions on usage is stronger for less experienced users, the relationship between long-term consequences and usage is stronger for more experienced users. In addition, the study shows that user experience is found to be directly and positively related to usage, in that more experienced users were using technology more than their inexperienced peers.

Innovation Diffusion Theory (IDT)

Drawing on the theory of innovation diffusion,[86] Moore and Benbasat[87] presented a model of perceptions of adopting an IT. Specifically, the model predicts that seven characteristics of innovations are instrumental in explaining why end users adopt a technological innovation. Table 2.9 presents these characteristics.

According to Moore and Benbasat,[88] relative advantage refers to "the degree to which an innovation is perceived as being better than its precursor"; ease of use is the degree to which an innovation is perceived as being easy to use; compatibility is the "the degree to which an innovation is perceived as being consistent with the existing values, needs, and past experiences of potential adopters"; image is "the degree to which use of an innovation is perceived to enhance one's image or status in one's social system." Additionally, visibility refers to the ability of an individual to

Table 2.9. The Innovation Diffusion Theory (IDT)

Predictors	Moderators	Outcome(s)
• Relative advantage	• Experience	• Innovation adoption
• Ease of use		
• Image		
• Visibility		
• Compatibility		
• Results demonstrability		
• Voluntariness of usage		

see other individuals using the system; results demonstrability refers to how tangible the results of using an innovation are, including their observability and communicability; and voluntariness of usage is defined as "the degree to which use of the innovation is perceived as being voluntary or of free will."

The empirical support offered in Moore and Benbasat's study shows that the seven characteristics are highly predictive of an employee's adoption of IT. Yet, in another study, it is found that user experience moderates the relationships between innovation characteristics and adoption and usage of IT.[89] Specifically, the study shows that prior to adoption of an IT, only relative advantage, ease of use, results demonstrability, and visibility predict adoption, whereas once the system is adopted by employees, system usage is predicted by only two characteristics, namely, relative advantage and image.

The Social Cognitive Model of Technology Usage (SCMTU)

Social cognitive theory (SCT) represents a widely accepted and empirically validated model of human behavior[90] that has also been applied in technology acceptance research. Specifically, Compeau and Higgins[91] adapt one basic notion of SCT, namely, self-efficacy, to the context of computer usage, with the aim of explaining why users actually make use of a system. Their model—the social cognitive model of technology usage (SCMTU)—which is presented in Table 2.10, predicts that (a) encouragement by others, (b) others' use, and (c) support predict computer self-efficacy and outcome expectations (i.e., job-related and personal outcome expectations). In addition, the authors posit that computer self-efficacy influences outcome expectations and, together, self-efficacy and outcome

Table 2.10. The Social Cognitive Model of Technology Usage (SCMTU)

Predictors	Mediators	Outcome(s)
• Encouragement by others • Others' use • Support	• Computer self-efficacy • Job-related outcome expectations • Personal outcome expectations	• Affect • Anxiety • Usage

expectations determine emotional reactions to computers (i.e., affect and anxiety) as well as actual computer usage.

Computer self-efficacy is defined as "a judgment of one's capability to use a computer."[92] Encouragement by others refers to verbal persuasion by people to whom an individual looks to obtain guidance to behavioral expectations. Others' use is defined as "the actual behavior of others with respect to the technology."[93] Support refers to availability of assistance to computer users by the organization. Outcome expectations are the expected consequences of computer usage and parallel the TAM-related notion of perceived usefulness. Outcome expectations are divided into two types of expectations: (a) job-related outcome expectations, which refer to performance expectations from using the computer, and (b) personal outcome expectations, which refer to the personal consequences of usage, such as esteem and sense of accomplishment. Affect refers to an individual's liking for a particular behavior, such as computer usage. Anxiety pertains to negative emotional reactions related to computer usage. Finally, computer usage is defined as the duration and frequency of using the computer.[94]

Compeau and Higgins[95] tested SCMTU with a large sample of managers and professionals. They found that computer self-efficacy represents an important individual trait en route to explaining technology usage. In particular, they found that computer self-efficacy was strongly related to (a) individuals' expectations of the outcomes of using computers, (b) anxiety, (c) affect, and (d) actual system usage. In addition, the study showed that encouragement by others, others' use of computers, and support positively influenced self-efficacy as well as both types of outcomes expectations.

Unified Theory of Acceptance and Use of Technology (UTAUT)

Based on a comprehensive review of the most prominent technology acceptance models, Venkatesh, Morris, Davis, and Davis[96] developed a unified model that integrates elements across models. The model is called the unified theory of acceptance and use of technology (UTAUT), and its elements are displayed in Table 2.11.

Table 2.11. The Unified Theory of Acceptance and Use of Technology (UTAUT)

Predictors	Mediators	Moderators	Outcome(s)
• Performance expectancy • Effort expectancy • Social influence • Facilitating conditions	• Behavioral intention	• Gender • Age • Experience • Voluntariness of use	• Use behavior

UTAUT posits that usage behavior is determined by behavioral intention, which is in turn influenced by four predictors: (a) performance expectancy, (b) effort expectancy, (c) social influence, and (d) facilitating conditions. However, facilitating conditions are also hypothesized to exert a direct influence on usage behavior. Finally, the model also predicts that gender, age, experience, and voluntariness of use are moderating the effects of the four predictors on behavioral intentions and usage behavior.

Performance expectancy is defined as "the degree to which an individual believes that using the system will help him or her to attain gains in job performance."[97] It is related to the notions of perceived usefulness, extrinsic motivation, job-fit relative advantage, and outcome expectations that have been advanced in prior technology acceptance models. Effort expectancy refers to "the degree of ease associated with the use of the system"[98] and is associated with the constructs of perceived ease of use and complexity. Social influence refers to "the degree to which an individual perceives that important others believe he or she should use the new system."[99] This construct is similar to subjective norms and social factors appearing in the TRA and MPCU models. Facilitating conditions relate to the "degree to which an individual believes that an organizational and technical infrastructure exists to support use of the system,"[100] and parallels the notions of perceived behavioral control and compatibility.

Venkatesh and colleagues[101] put UTAUT under empirical scrutiny, and the results of their research efforts suggest that UTAUT outperforms any other technology acceptance model both under voluntary and mandatory usage settings. In particular, the study shows that the four predictors are strongly related to behavioral intentions to use an IT. However, the study also shows that important moderating mechanisms are in place. Specifically, the effects of performance expectancy on intentions become stronger for men and as age increases. In contrast, effort expectancy has a stronger influence on intentions when employees are female and older and a weaker influence as experience increases. Moreover, the relationship between facilitating conditions and intentions is stronger when age and experience increase. Finally, social influence appears to be related to intentions when usage is mandatory, with increased levels of age, and for female employees. Given its parsimonious nature and explanatory power, UTAUT holds the potential of helping researchers and practitioners understand and manage the process of technology acceptance in organizations. Indeed, supportive evidence of the model's validity and predictability across contexts and cultures has been accumulated in recent years.[102]

Comparison of Technology Acceptance Models

Each of the 10 technology acceptance and use models described provides a theory-based perspective regarding how technologies are accepted and used by employees. While each has its own merit and employs a different theoretical lens, a common theme underlying most models is that a set of factors (or predictors) influences employees' intentions to use an IT that are, in turn, influencing actual technology usage. These sets of influencing factors can be grouped into four categories:

1. System characteristics
2. Individual differences
3. Organizational influences
4. Environmental/contextual/industry factors

While this categorization does not attempt to build a new theory of technology acceptance and use, it nevertheless provides a useful and practical groundwork to researchers and executives interested in studying and managing sales technology implementation. This is so because the categories cover the entire gamut of influences on sales technology acceptance. Further evidence on their relevance to technology acceptance comes from prior studies that have employed similar nomenclatures to categorize the effects of internal and external environmental factors on information technology implementation.[103] On the basis of this categorization, the next chapter represents an effort to summarize the factors falling into each one of these four categories and to elaborate on their managerial implications for effective sales technology implementation.

Summary

By drawing on several lines of theory and research, we demonstrated that the sales technology implementation process comprises several stages, each of which should be carefully managed. Importantly, adoption or acceptance of the technology is just one—though important—stage in this process. Accordingly, we elaborated on several theoretical models of information technology acceptance by individual users. Based on these models, we uncovered four distinct categories of factors that might exert a significant influence on the acceptance of sales technologies.

CHAPTER 3

Antecedents to Effective Implementation

Chapter Overview

The previous chapter provided a detailed theoretical overview of the various models of technology acceptance and use. With the aim of helping practicing managers use this knowledge in the most efficient manner, the present chapter represents an effort to systematically organize the extant literature regarding the antecedents of effective implementation into a set of managerially useful categories (see Figure 3.1). To this end, we draw not only on the aforementioned models but also on several other lines of inquiry. Given that the proposed categorization represents a summary abstraction of a vast amount of knowledge into a few higher-order categories, it is parsimonious. It can, therefore, provide the basis for a systematic analysis of the implementation process of sales technologies. Specifically, the categories are organized around four themes. The first theme relates to the characteristics of the system; the second theme relates to characteristics of the individual users; the third theme refers to concepts that deal with the wider organizational context; and, finally the fourth theme refers to external influences stemming mainly from a firm's environment and market situation.

As seen from Figure 3.1, the four categories of antecedents to technology implementation are *interrelated*. That means that the influence of a category on implementation is not taking place in a vacuum; rather, it influences, and is influenced, by factors falling into the other categories in such a way that it may be naïve to expect that only a subset of factors will influence implementation. Indeed, as was evident from the review of the major technology acceptance-use models presented in the previous chapter, users may accept or reject an information technology due to the

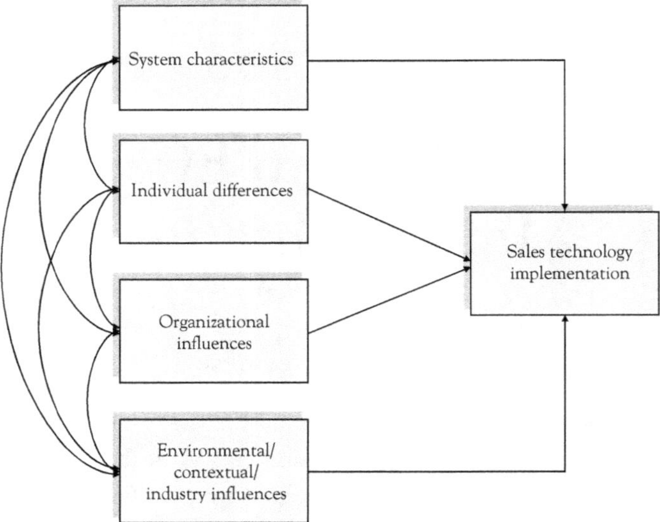

Figure 3.1. Antecedents to effective sales technology implementation.

joint influence of several factors, such as the organizational environment and the characteristics of the technology. The next sections detail the factors comprising each of the four categories, with the aim of providing managers with useful knowledge regarding effective implementation of a sales technology.

System Characteristics

System characteristics are the inherent characteristics and attributes of the sales technology. The related literature on innovation adoption offers many suggestions as to which characteristics of a technological innovation (e.g., SFA) are inducing users to accept and make use of it.[1] For practicing managers, this entails that they have to be extremely careful when selecting vendors, since solutions and their characteristics can vary greatly across different suppliers. Table 3.1 lists the most pertinent of these characteristics as well as their descriptions.

The first system characteristic refers to communicability, which is defined as the degree to which aspects of an innovation may be conveyed to others.[2] This notion is very similar to observability, that is, the degree to which the results of an innovation are visible to others.[3] Nevertheless,

Table 3.1. System Characteristics Influencing Technology Acceptance and Usage

Factor	Description
Communicability[6]	The degree to which aspects of an innovation may be conveyed to others.[7]
Compatibility[8]	The degree to which an innovation is perceived as being consistent with the existing values, past experiences, and needs of the receivers.[9]
Complexity[10]	The degree to which an innovation is perceived as relatively difficult to understand and use.[11]
Information accuracy[12]	The degree of accurate information on customers that a sales technology provides.
Observability[13]	The degree to which the results of an innovation are visible to others.[14]
Perceived ease of use[15]	The degree to which an individual believes that using a particular system would be free of physical and mental effort.[16]
Perceived usefulness[17]	The degree to which an individual believes that using a particular system will enhance his or her job performance.[18]
Perceived voluntariness[19]	The extent to which potential adopters perceive the adoption decision to be nonmandated.[20]
Person-technology fit[21]	The degree to which the technology is consistent with one's job and profession.[22]
Relative advantage[23]	The degree to which an innovation is perceived as being better than the idea it supersedes.[24]
Social approval[25]	The status gained in one's reference group—a nonfinancial aspect of reward.[26]
Trialability[27]	The degree to which an innovation may be experimented with on a limited basis.[28]

the implication is that for effective adoption of an IT, employees need to see the results of adopting the system. Simply put, if management has not communicated the resulting benefits of IT usage, salespeople will be reluctant to make use of the system.

Perhaps the most studied innovation characteristic is compatibility, which is assumed to positively affect acceptance. The rationale is that a technology that fits with already existent processes, technologies, and employees' personal values and needs will be accepted more easily by members of the organization. This is very important in a sales force context, given that salespeople usually dislike changes that call on learning new things and changing already established procedures that have proven effective in the past.

An innovation should not be complex to use, thus minimizing a user's perception of the time and effort needed to properly master the technology.[4] This is very important since salespeople are paid for their accomplishments, which depend largely on their expended effort and time spent on selling. If sales technology consumes a disproportional amount of their time, salespeople will view the technology as a foe rather than a friend and will tend to underutilize it.

Sales is an information-intensive profession, in the sense that salespeople rely on the timeliness and accuracy of customer information to make decisions and perform their roles. As such, it is very important that the information that is provided to salespeople through sales technologies needs to be relevant and of maximum quality. If this is not the case, then users may feel that the system is not useful for their jobs, and they will thus reject it. There is nothing more frustrating for a salesperson than a database full of errors regarding the potential of sales leads and customer contact information, including customer demographic profiles. This consumes valuable time from salespeople's main selling activities, thereby leading them to distrust the IT. For instance, one study has shown that when customer information is not perceived as accurate, then it is least likely that users will accept the system.[5]

Two perceptions—which originate from TAM conceptualization as major influences of how salespeople view sales technology—are "perceived usefulness" (a notion similar to relative advantage) and "perceived ease of use" (a notion similar to complexity). Numerous studies that have been conducted in the sales literature have provided evidence that the two perceptions can strongly affect behavioral intentions or actual behavior concerning technology usage.[29]

Managerially speaking, the two perceptions imply that the sales force has to visualize the intended benefits of using the system, such as increases in selling time and productivity and decreases in administrative work. Since mastering a sales technology can consume a significant amount of a salesperson's time, firms also need to ensure that users have positive perceptions of the technology in order for them to invest time and effort in learning the system.[30] Importantly, the degree to which a system is perceived as useful or easy to use may vary greatly between management and the sales force, thus leading to less-than-desired acceptance levels.[31] As such, managers should assess sales force perceptions regarding what they consider as useful and easy to use in their daily work routines. This must be done early in the process of implementation by running a short survey or by interviewing salespeople regarding their expectations. If large differences between management and sales force perceptions are uncovered, interventions should be made in order to alleviate any concerns that salespeople may have regarding the technology. In addition, management may wish to consider involving salespeople in the buying decision-making process, since such an action will signal that the company cares for salespeople's needs and will increase affective commitment to the project. Also, managers should note that the effects of perceived usefulness and ease of use may be different depending on the stage of the implementation process. Specifically, one study has shown that perceived usefulness has stronger effects during preimplementation (i.e., when measuring intentions of using a sales technology) rather than postimplementation, where actual use is considered.[32]

The degree to which use of an innovation is perceived as mandatory (or not) can also influence its acceptance rate among targeted users. This notion has been referred to as "perceived voluntariness,"[33] a perception that can vary greatly among users. When individuals perceive an innovation to be voluntary—as opposed to being mandatory—they tend to hold positive attitudes toward the innovation and consequently make full use of it.[34]

Speier and Venkatesh[35] have enriched the related literature by adding another system characteristic, namely, "person-technology fit," which can influence adoption decision. Person-technology fit, that is, the degree to which the technology is consistent with one's professional and organizational role identities,[36] can positively influence usage of a sales technology. When salespeople perceive that the technology enhances both their job performance (i.e., job fit) and their long-term career opportunities (i.e., professional fit), then they are more likely to have positive attitudes toward the technology, and, as such, they will tend to use the system to a greater extent. Speier and Venkatesh argue that the positive impact of person-technology fit is rooted in the competence-enhancing mechanisms that stem from technology usage. Thus, managers should strive to ensure that salespeople view technologies as "enablers" that enrich the values of existing competences and relationships.

Finally, two perceptions that can influence adoption are "social approval" and trialability. The first concept implies that employees may adopt a technology if it positively affects their professional image and status among peers, supervisors, and customers. Trialability—the degree to which potential users are given the opportunity to experiment and try a technology during the planning or installation phases of the implementation process, prior committing to its usage—has also been found to positively affect adoption.[37]

Individual Differences

Individual-user characteristics (or individual differences) can play an important role in effective IT implementation.[38] Consequently, this section is concerned with delineating some of the most prominent characteristics that have been discussed in the extant literature (see Table 3.2). To facilitate understanding of these characteristics, we distinguish between two subcategories of individual differences: (a) demographic factors and (b) psychographic factors.

Demographic factors, such as age, education, and prior technology experience, may exert influence on a salesperson's tendency to use a sales technology. Generally speaking, salespeople who are younger, less experienced, better educated, but more experienced with technology usage, will be more inclined to adopt the technology since they are usually more familiar with new technologies and feel more confident using them.[39] In contrast, older, more experienced salespeople have accumulated knowledge and developed successful selling tactics through the years that they are less willing to abandon absent a compelling reason.[40] In addition, more experienced salespeople who are not so productive may view technology as a threat to make them obsolete.[41]

Another demographic trait that has received limited attention in prior research is gender. In general, the evidence from a small number of studies shows that women are more resistant to new technologies and tend to have more negative perceptions toward IT when compared to men.[42] Therefore, when launching sales technologies, managers need to provide more support to older salespeople, who are presumably not so well educated and have less prior experience with related technologies, and to women, who may not be so positively predisposed toward technology.

Table 3.2. Individual Differences Influencing Technology Acceptance and Usage

Factor	Description
Demographic	
Age[43]	The age of the salesperson.
Education[44]	Years of formal education.
Prior technology experience[45]	Years of prior experience with related technology.
Gender[46]	The gender of the salesperson.
Psychographic	
Computer playfulness[47]	The degree of cognitive spontaneity in microcomputer interactions, where a high level of cognitive spontaneity indicates a high degree of playfulness, and a low level of cognitive spontaneity indicates a low degree of playfulness.[48]
Computer self-efficacy[49]	A judgment of one's capability to use a computer.[50]
Fear of being isolated	The negative emotional state associated with an individual's anticipation of sales technology allowing for isolation from company life.
Fear of being monitored[51]	The negative emotional state associated with an individual's anticipation of sales technology allowing for invasion of privacy.
Fear of losing job[52]	The negative emotional state associated with an individual's anticipation of sales technology allowing for replacement of one's job.
Fear of losing power[53]	The negative emotional state associated with an individual's anticipation of sales technology allowing for loss of organizational power.
Job satisfaction[54]	All characteristics of the job itself and the work environment which (industrial) salesmen find rewarding, fulfilling, and satisfying, or frustrating and unsatisfying.[55]
Learning orientation[56]	An individual's concern to increase his/her competence.[57]
Performance orientation[58]	An individual's concern to gain favorable judgment of his/her competence.[59]
Personal innovativeness[60]	The willingness of an individual to try out any new information technology.[61]
Resistance to change[62]	The extent to which organizational members hold positive views about the need for organizational change, as well as their belief that changes are likely to have positive implications for them and the organization.[63]
Technology-related role ambiguity[64]	The degree to which an individual salesperson is uncertain about using the SFA software.
Technology-related role conflict[65]	The degree to which an individual salesperson faces conflicting demands about using the SFA software.

Some users of information systems can draw satisfaction from the immediate intellectual development of a topic, such as interacting and using a computer. Those users consider usage as a joyful activity, and they tend to make more use of computers compared with other individuals who either feel anxiety with using computers or just dislike using technology. This tendency of individuals to feel joy with using computers is termed "computer playfulness."[66] Playfulness has been found to increase adoption of sales technology.[67]

It is common knowledge that one of the most "technophobic" occupational groups is the sales force.[68] Salespeople have traditionally disliked new technologies, and the level of technology utilization in the sales organization has been low. While younger and more educated salespeople are more predisposed toward technological applications in a work setting, some salespeople still fear them.[69] One basic source of this technophobia stems from their perceived incapableness to operate new technologies that makes them to resist their use. This perception is known as "computer self-efficacy" and is concerned with an individual judgment about whether she or he can use computer technology to perform her or his job tasks.[70] It is because of this type of fear that organizations must provide adequate levels of training and technical support during the entire lifetime of the implementation project. Some other researchers have proposed that technology self-efficacy is fundamental in explaining why users accept or resist sales technologies.[71] This proposition draws from self-efficacy theory,[72] which states that when users possess no prior experience, their confidence in their technology-related abilities will serve as a basis for the users' judgment regarding how difficult or easy a new system will be to use. Thus, users who believe that they possess higher levels of technological self-efficacy will try harder and be more persistent than individuals scoring lower on self-efficacy.[73]

The introduction of a sales technology can instill fears among members of a sales force. Generally speaking, a fear is a negative emotional state that is associated with the anticipation of occurrence of an unpleasant event. In the context of sales technology implementation, we propose that these fears can take four forms. First, technology may heighten salespeople's fears of being isolated from what is going on inside the company. The advent of mobile and wireless connectivity modules, which are embedded in many sales technology applications, has pushed salespeople away from being physically present in their firms' headquarters. Consider, for instance, a salesperson spending her day making calls to customers. In the past, the salesperson would go back to company headquarters to meet and interact with her supervisor in order to discuss sales results, share customer contact details, and design new strategies. Today, with the availability of wireless devices (utilizing third generation [3G] networks and voice over Internet protocol [VoIP] technologies), the salesperson does not have to return to the office.[74] She just has to upload the data by using the wireless device, regardless of whether she is on the road or at home. She can make a cell phone call or log into the company's portal to learn news and get the latest information on company strategy. This has, however, diminished the opportunity for being socialized and for getting together with peers and supervisors—a very important characteristic of social life in sales organizations.[75] Interaction is vital for keeping employees up to date with company developments and for increasing feelings of team coherence and organizational commitment. In fact, recent studies have provided evidence that perceptions of salesperson isolation negatively affect trust in supervisors and coworkers.[76] The isolation of a salesperson from a company's social life may even be more important, considering that many salespeople are remotely located from company offices and their opportunities for being connected to the company's life is diminished because of sales technology.

Sales technologies have enlarged a firm's capability to collect real-time information about employees' activities and to track the behaviors of individual salespeople.[77] For instance, firms are now capable of recording the number of sales calls, sales tactics being used for each account, and the performance of each account along the sales cycle. While management may receive this as a formidable opportunity to exercise better control and micromanagement, salespeople may not feel the same about it. Technology enables management to monitor salespeople's conversations, behaviors, and activities through such technologies as cell phones, global positioning system (GPS) devices, and sales force automation (SFA) systems. This, however, can give rise to the second type of technology-related fear, namely "fear of being monitored." Salespeople's fear of being surveilled by management was never so heightened than it is since sales technologies have entered the world of sales. In many instances, this fear of being monitored through advanced technology has given rise to what has been called the "big brother" syndrome in modern sales.[78] The enhanced ability of management to control the activities of salespeople has limited one idiosyncratic characteristic of the sales job: autonomy and independence.[79] As such, a segment of the sales force may feel threatened by technology to the extent that they perceive it as a tool for allowing management to intrude on their privacy.[80] Therefore, management should very carefully and unambiguously articulate how, and under what circumstances, information regarding salespeople's behaviors will be collected, stored, and monitored, and how information will help the firm to improve the sales process.[81] Communicating the policies of the organization regarding information use should involve both top management announcements and planned supervisor-salesperson interactions during sales meetings.

The third type of fear may be associated with an individual's negative emotion that the sales technology has been implemented in order to replace her or him, thereby heightening job insecurity concerns.[82] Although this may not accurately reflect reality, some salespeople may feel threatened by technology if they view it as a competitive force and not as a supplement to their activities. Simply put, the value of the sales technology is in the eye of the beholder. Some salespeople will positively view technology, but many will have difficulties in anticipating how technology will affect their jobs, especially when technology is being implemented to facilitate transactions at the company-customer interface level, as is the case with EDI or other electronic-channel additions to current sales strategy. In some extreme situations, some salespeople may be tempted to sabotage the implementation effort to save their jobs.[83] Therefore, it is vital that management spells out, to the letter, policies regarding how technology is embedded into the wider strategy of the organization, how it will affect the jobs and lives of individual salespeople, and how the sales force will continue to create value for the firm.

Finally, implementation of a sales technology implies that salespeople are called on to share hard-earned information about customers, markets, and competitors or their list of leads, contacts, and customers.[84] However, one of the main sources of power that salespeople possess in organizations is precisely their ability to know more of what is going on in the market compared with management. Salespeople develop close relationships with their customers and get to know much about their needs and idiosyncratic characteristics. Consequently, many customers are more loyal to salespeople rather than to firms,[85] a situation that makes salespeople feel that they "own" the customer.[86] This gives salespeople the power to negotiate with supervisors, exert pressure on new policies, and develop an image of irreplacebility within the company. Management interventions that ask salespeople to disclose intimate information with the rest of the company may promote fears of losing power because doing so can threaten a salesperson's expert status.[87] As a consequence, many salespeople may resist sharing proprietary information and keep on recording it on private databases that they maintain on their own.[88] A plausible solution to this problem is positioning the sales technology as a tool for increasing sales force productivity and not as a managerial effort to take over salespeople's relationships with their customers.[89]

Research evidence shows that salespeople who exhibit higher levels of job satisfaction are more likely to accept new technologies, since they feel better with their work, peers, supervisor, and company.[90] These positive feelings toward the company will reduce resistance and make salespeople adopt the technology.

Salespeople can pursue two broad types of goals in their work. The first is learning orientation, whereby employees value the feelings of personal growth, enjoy learning new things, and seek to improve their competences; the second is performance orientation, where employees are reluctant to experiment with new approaches in their job and look to achieve a favorable evaluation of their current abilities and level of performance from important others.[91] Accordingly, the goal orientations of salespeople can also impact their decision to adopt a technology. Recent research shows that both orientations are positively related to adopting behavior, with neither being more important than the other. The authors argue that due to idiosyncratic characteristics of their job, salespeople simultaneously seek to learn new things and to be effective. On the basis of the study's findings, managers are advised to foster an implementation environment that signals how the new technology can help salespeople to master new skills and improve their performances.[92]

The tendency of a salesperson to accept new technologies may also be influenced by her personal innovativeness, a relatively stable trait of an individual's personality. In general, innovative individuals are those who adopt innovations earlier than other people in a given social system.[93]

However, within the context of IT, personal innovativeness is defined as the "willingness of an individual to try out any new information technology."[94]

Several explanations can be offered as to why innovative individuals will tend to make use of sales technology. First, innovative individuals are generally keen of new ideas, processes, tools, and methods, and they tend to exhibit the lowest level of resistance to anything new to their company or to their own job. As such, it is also more likely that they will be among the first to adopt and use a sales technology.[95] Second, innovative individuals usually seek out information regarding an innovation from multiple sources, a situation that increases their familiarity with the innovation; thus, they are more likely to accept it.[96] Conversely, individuals who are not innovative will tend to experience considerable levels of job stress due to the increased need for change that is brought with the introduction of technology.[97] Finally, another explanation is that innovative individuals will either exhibit more positive attitudes toward the technology or use it on the basis of prior habits.[98]

All in all, personal innovativeness appears to be very important in urging individuals to accept or resist a given technology.[99] In fact, as one study has shown, innovativeness may be particularly relevant in explaining why technologies are utilized to a different extent even within the same organization.[100] As such, the construct of "innovativeness" can be employed by managers to identify employees that will most probably adopt the technology earlier than colleagues. These employees may serve as "change agents," in general, or "sales technology champions," in specific, and stimulate usage among members of the sales organization. Our practical experience with sales technology implementations, however, leads us to conclude that salespeople with an innovative attitude should not normally make up the majority in an organization.

The introduction of a sales technology is accompanied by changes in work routines. If salespeople fail to see the connection between technology and their ability to better sell to and serve customers, resistance will most probably kick in the process of implementation.[101] Thus, several authors have contemplated that managing technology implementation should be viewed as a planned change initiative that aims to minimize resistance to change.[102] According to Kwahk and Lee,[103] the underlying mechanism is that users will be inclined to use the technology only if they find it useful and easy to use, factors that are, in turn, influenced by readiness for change. Thus, Kwahk and Lee recommend that firms influence users' readiness for change by increasing (a) users' organizational commitment, that is, "the relative strength of an individual's identification with, and involvement in, a particular organization,"[104] and (b) users' perceived personal competence, that is, "the degree of the individual's feelings of competence in the work role."[105]

Under certain situations, a sales technology can also increase role stress, which can have dysfunctional consequences for the performance of salespeople.[106] Two of the most heavily studied role stressors related to a salesperson's job are role ambiguity (i.e., a stress situation in which a salesperson lacks clear direction about the expectations of his or her role in the job or organization) and role conflict (i.e., the degree to which work expectations and work requirements of two or more persons are incompatible).[107] As Rangarajan, Jones, and Chin[108] have shown, salespeople may feel either uncertain about using technology (i.e., technology-related role ambiguity) or that the technology is in conflict with other sales activities and job demands (i.e., technology-related role conflict). Because sales technology introduces profound changes to a salesperson's role responsibilities (e.g., by adding new sales activities), the salesperson may experience heightened levels of role-related stress. When this happens, the salesperson may expend less effort integrating the sales technology into her daily job activities,[109] or she may feel that the system is incompatible with prior systems[110] and thus not make full use of the system. Consequently, managers are advised to very carefully consider how the new technology impacts salespeople's roles and to plan actions that will alleviate role stress.

Organizational Influences

The extant literature is very rich in terms of prescribing factors that are related to attributes of the organization and that might influence the acceptance and usage of an IT. To facilitate discussion and knowledge advancement, we categorize these attributes into three types: (a) management practices and processes, (b) structural characteristics, and (c) culture. Table 3.3 lists a representative sample of factors falling into each type of organizational influence.

Table 3.3. Organizational Influences on Technology Acceptance and Usage

Factor	Description
Management practices and processes	
Implementation climate[126]	Targeted employees' shared summary perceptions of the extent to which their use of a specific innovation is rewarded, supported, and expected within their organization.[127]
Top management support[128]	The CEO's activities or substantive personal interventions in the management of IT.[129]
Technical support[130]	Extent of providing company-sponsored, formalized technical support to end-users when problems with using the sales technology occur.
Training[131]	Extent of providing company-sponsored, formalized training programs to end-users on how to use the sales technology.
Incentive systems[132]	Organizational decisions concerning the type and level of incentives in the compensation package of salespeople.
Planning[133]	Development of a formalized planning procedure for sales technology implementation.
User participation[134]	The behaviors, assignments, and activities that users or their representatives perform during the information system development process.[135]
Communication of the implementation process[136]	Organizational activities and actions aimed at communicating the objectives and the expectations of the sales technology initiative to targeted users.
Change management[137]	Formalized activities undertaken in order to manage change that is brought by the introduction of technology.
Business process orientation[138]	The degree to which an organization designs and implements processes, activities, and tasks to create customer value.[139]
Structural characteristics	
Centralization[140]	The degree to which power and control in a system are concentrated in the hands of relatively few individuals.[141]
Formalization[142]	The degree to which an organization emphasizes following rules and procedures in the role performance of its members.[143]
Interdepartmental relationships[144]	The extent of coordination, cooperation, information exchange, resource dependence, and structural links among a firm's functional units.

Table 3.3. Organizational Influences on Technology Acceptance and Usage (cont.)

Factor	Description
Culture	
Customer orientation[145]	The set of beliefs that puts the customer's interest first, while not excluding those of all other stakeholders such as owners, managers, and employees, in order to develop a long-term profitable enterprise.[146]
Organizational innovativeness[147]	The degree to which users perceive the organization to be open to new products and ideas.

Developing an appropriate climate for implementation is generally recognized as a critical activity for technology adoption and usage. According to Klein and Sorra, implementation climate refers to "targeted employees' shared summary perceptions of the extent to which their use of a specific innovation is rewarded, supported, and expected within their organization."[111] Given this definition, it is obvious that climate represents an umbrella term that comprises several variables, such as training, rewarding, and support.[112]

Gaining the support of top management (e.g., CEO or C-level managers) early in the process is critical for ensuring that employees will accept the technology.[113] Support from senior management acts like a signal that conveys a picture of importance to the sales force through committed resources and leadership.[114] If top management is not committed to the implementation effort, it is less likely that the sales force will apply the effort needed to make use of the system. Consequently, it is imperative to secure that top management is supporting the system in order for successful implementation to occur. For instance, management can employ the organization's communication systems to educate potential users on what the organization expects from system usage, what the intended benefits are, and how the organization can achieve its objectives by using the system.

Providing technical support to users when problems arise appears to be another critical issue in the implementation process.[115] Upon starting to use a system, users may be confronted with a myriad of problems, ranging from understanding basic functionalities to wireless connection "blackouts." Thus, the perceived time and effort needed to master a given system may be prolonged and the learning process may be irrevocably hurt.[116] If these problems are not resolved, users may feel frustrated or may feel that the system does not fit their current level of competence. In this case, they will tend to reject it. As such, providing hands-on support to users, especially to novice ones who may not have the experience or the required knowledge to overcome these problems, is imperative in order to ease the learning process and increase the system's perceived ease of use and usefulness. Technical support can be provided through several means, such as online or help-desk facilities, and, ideally, should be available on a 24-hour basis.

Training users how to use the system and how to integrate it into their current work practices is critically important for successful implementation, as evidenced in a great number of studies.[117] Training can stimulate usage by minimizing risk, ambiguity, and uncertainty surrounding the impact of the technology on salespeople, and by showing salespeople the technology's upside. Moreover, training can help salespeople develop the necessary knowledge to make full use of the system. If users are not trained to confront the new work reality, adoption and subsequent use is not going to occur at the desired levels. In one study, for instance, it was found that the absence of training is one of the most common SFA pitfalls in organizations that were not found to have accomplished their automation goals.[118] Consequently, organizations need to provide formalized, organization-sponsored sales technology training that will meet the varying needs of the sales force.[119] Training can take the form of either general computing skills or specific knowledge and understanding of the sales technology being implemented.[120] However, training has to be an ongoing process, starting prior to a sales technology's roll out and continuing during the entire lifetime of system implementation.[121]

Some authors have advocated that technology usage needs to be linked with a firm's incentive system in order to ensure successful implementation.[122] The rationale is that most field salespeople are very careful in allocating their time to different activities in order to maximize their personal income. If the link between system usage and their compensation is not apparent, then they may be very reluctant to make use of the system, since they may view technology as another onerous task that consumes their time and minimizes chances for earning more money. The sparse empirical literature on the subject shows that tying compensation to usage is beneficial. Specifically, one study shows not only that an increase in the level of incentives is positively associated with individuals' technology usage but also that outcome-based incentives (i.e., incentives related to an individual's end results) have greater effects on technology usage compared with behavior-based incentives (i.e., incentives related to an individual's behaviors).[123] These findings are consistent with the results of another study that showed that an outcome-based control or compensation system is associated with higher levels of sales technology adoption.[124] Accordingly, managers should consider providing some form of financial incentives to salespeople for using sales technologies when this is, of course, in alignment with the overall compensation policy. However, there might be a risk in tying usage to compensation since salespeople could be monitoring and manipulating usage in order to gain their bonuses.[125]

Ideally, the sales technology implementation should involve extensive planning efforts. The first step in this process is to set specific objectives for the sales technology in accordance with the company's own needs.[148] For instance, one firm may choose to set the objective of implementing the technology to increase customer response time, whereas another firm may choose to decrease time spent on administrative activities. In developing objectives, managers should keep in mind that goals must be measurable in order to facilitate the development of relevant metrics. Developing metrics is a very important part of the planning process, but it can be especially difficult when objectives are more qualitative or intangible, like increasing customer satisfaction. Effectively setting objectives, however, should involve a detailed analysis of firm's needs regarding technology and information. Managers might employ a blueprint approach to map how sales technology is influencing the sales process.[149] Then, based on this analysis, managers should set objectives and develop a plan of what is going to be automated and what information needs to be collected in order to fulfill firm's objectives. In addition, sales managers need to craft a customer strategy that will guide the whole process.[150] Customer strategy refers to the organizational processes for developing, growing, and managing customer relationships that have to be linked to the sales technology.

The salesperson is the targeted user and, ultimately, the "internal customer" of most sales technologies.[151] As such, her voice should be heard early in the implementation process when evaluating and selecting vendors.[152] Input from the sales force can be collected through meetings, surveys, and interviews.[153] Involving salespeople in the implementation process tends to promote a sense of inclusion and interest representation, thereby increasing feelings of ownership.[154] When users feel they have played a part in the implementation effort, they tend to comprehend the objectives of the implementation, develop realistic expectations about system capabilities, and have a more positive attitude toward the system than users who have not participated. As such, users feel that the whole process is fairer and that the organization cares for their interests, something that can immensely increase chances of a smooth implementation. In fact, one meta-analytic study provided evidence of this, showing that employee participation in the implementation process is the most important factor in effective implementation.[155] However, it is unfortunate that, in many instances, the sales force has no place in the buying decision process, thereby leading to high levels of resistance.

Another way to look at the introduction of a sales technology is through a change-management lens. Given that sales technology disturbs current sales force practices and changes the way activities are performed, or introduces new activities, sales management should make intense efforts to persuade the sales force that the change is beneficial. This may be accomplished through enacting organizational change processes.[156] One such process refers to involving the sales force early in the implementation process or by communicating accurate and timely information regarding the initiative.[157] Through two-way communication, targeted users feel they have control over the situation, which helps in garnering consensus prior to implementation and in creating an internal environment that favors the acceptance of new ideas and work practices.[158] The role of participation and communication in successful, planned change implementation has been documented in a recent study.[159] Specifically, the study showed that participation and communication positively affected employees' subjective norms and perceived behavioral control, and subsequently, employee's intention to accept change. Communication efforts should also target spelling out what the organization expects from salespeople after the introduction of the new technology.[160] Users must have a clear set of expectations regarding how the system will be used, how it will help them perform their job better, and what the expected impact of the system on their performance is. Too many times, firms focus on technological features instead of demonstrating the benefits of automation for the sales force, thereby increasing ambiguity. Communication can help members of the sales force to shape positive perceptions regarding the new technology.[161] This can help the organization to minimize role inaccuracy and to make the connection between technology usage and performance clearer.

Firms implementing sales technologies should consider whether changes are required in organizational processes and systems, such as compensation, training, and organizational structure.[162] Given that sales technology often disrupts current working processes and calls for integration of different functional units, some authors have advocated that business-process orientation is an important element of successful implementation.[163] This involves the precise definition of processes that may span functional silos and that have an impact on building, maintaining, and developing customer relationships.

Organizational structure may play an important role in technology acceptance. The extant literature identifies two particularly useful dimensions that managers need to consider when implementing a technology: centralization and formalization.[164] Specifically, during the initial stages of implementation, when firms become aware of their need to adopt a specific technology, to collect information about potential vendors, and to buy the technology, lower levels of formalization and centralization may be preferred over a more mechanistic and centralized organizational structure.[165] This is because participative decision making, less emphasis on hierarchy, and a flexible and open system facilitate information accessibility.[166] However, higher levels of centralization and formalization may be needed during later stages of the implementation process, since a tighter, more mechanistic, and more centralized structure can reduce role ambiguity and role conflict and expedite implementation.[167] Thus, when power is centralized and organizations have put well-defined standard operating procedures for technology use into action, employees will tend to use the technology more, thereby resulting in higher implementation rates.

Within the context of structural characteristics, the nature of interdepartmental relationships (i.e., the extent of coordination, cooperation, information exchange, resource dependence, and structural links among

units) should play an important role in facilitating technology implementation. For instance, task dependence—which refers to the extent to
which two units depend on each other for assistance, information, compliance, or other coordinative acts in the performance of their respective
tasks[168]—may increase technology diffusion within organizations. This
is so because different units, which are highly dependent on each other
in order to perform their respective tasks, will tend to use the same technologies.[169] A higher degree of interdepartmental connectedness (i.e., the
degree of formal and informal direct contact among employees across
departments) and a low degree of interdepartmental conflict (i.e., the
tension among departments arising from the incompatibility of actual
or desired responses)[170] may also influence the diffusion of technologies
since both can induce the exchange of information and facilitate communication.[171] Sales managers will need to realize that implementing a
sales technology, such as a sales-based customer relationship management (CRM) system, is not function specific but rather a team effort that
should involve other departments—besides sales—such as marketing,
operations, accounting, customer service, and IT.[172]

Culture should play a role in facilitating technology acceptance as
well. Though a firm's culture is comprised of many different values, two
are most prominent in a sales technology context. First, implementation
of sales technologies ultimately aims at improving customer satisfaction
as well as the ability of salespeople to build better relationships with key
customers. All too often, however, organizational policies and practices
work contrary to this objective and primarily serve to attain efficiency
or productivity gains. If the organization has not established a customer-
centric culture, which emphasizes the importance of customers for sur-
vival, then it is least likely that members of the sales organization will
use the technology.[173] Conversely, organizations whose cultures signal
a strong customer-centric message will tend to highly value customers
and thus establish a set of values and norms for improving customers'
performance, through acquiring and using knowledge about customers
and their needs. In such organizations, salespeople look for customer
information in multiple units of the organization that can help them
better perform their job. Consequently, organizations with a customer-
centric culture will experience higher rates of sales technology usage and
a smoother transition to the new working reality. Based on this line of

reasoning, firms need to foster a market orientation, which places the customer at the heart of all the firm's activities, in order to facilitate technology adoption and usage.

A second value comprising a firm's culture is organizational innovativeness. If users perceive the organization to be open to new ideas, processes, and technologies, they will be socially prompted to comply with innovative norms and will tend to more easily accept a sales technology as part of their job, even if they are not so innovative themselves.[174]

Environmental/Contextual/Industrial Influences

The last category of influences on sales technology implementation stems from a firm's environment and context and can have severe impact on the success of technology implementation (see Table 3.4). In particular, several authors have proposed that at least some dimensions of a firm's external environment, such as market and technological turbulence, as well as competitive intensity, may lead to higher rates of intraorganizational diffusion of technologies.[175] The general rationale is that under

Table 3.4. Environmental/Contextual/Industrial Influences on Technology Acceptance/Usage

Factor	Description
Market turbulence[183]	The rate of change in the composition of customers and their preferences.[184]
Technological turbulence[185]	The rate of technological change.[186]
Competitive intensity[187]	The level of direct competition that the focal firm faces within its immediate business domain.[188]
Customer pressure[189]	The degree to which customers expect salespeople to utilize sales technology.
Competitive pressure[190]	The degree to which competitive salespeople utilize sales technology.
Peer pressure[191]	The degree to which other salespeople in the organization utilize sales technology.
Superiors' influence[192]	The degree to which a salesperson's superiors use and support sales technology.
Task-technology fit[193]	The degree to which a technology assists an individual in performing his or her portfolio of tasks.[194]

a more unpredictable and dynamic environment, where customer preferences change quickly and the ability to accurately forecast demand is diminished, firms structure their internal processes in such a way so as to induce innovation adoption.[176] In addition, competitive intensity may be conducive to technology adoption, at least to some extent, since a hostile environment in which competitive advantage can quickly become a commodity urges firms to seek to differentiate themselves through innovation.[177] Consequently, salespeople who are particularly responsive to market and competitive signals will be more inclined to adopt and use sales technologies when they perceive a highly dynamic, turbulent, and competitive environment.

Other contextual influences may stem from a focal salesperson's social environment.[178] Specifically, the degree to which salespeople perceive their customers, peers, superiors, and salespeople in competing firms to either utilize or expect the usage of sales technology, may have a strong and positive influence on their decision to adopt and use the technology.[179] This rationale draws on the notion of "subjective norms" in the TRA, as well as on the simple observation that salespeople are operating within the boundaries of the organization; as such, signals from important others (e.g., competition and customers) can have a severe effect on their decision to use sales technology. Specifically, customers may already use technology or demand that salespeople use technology; given that salespeople are responsive to customer needs, salespeople will respond to customer signals and use sales technologies.[180] In addition, the utilization of technologies by competitive salespeople may serve as a stepping-stone for salespeople to make use of a sales technology in order to sustain their competitive advantage and professional image in the market and avoid facing opportunity costs. Likewise, the social fabric of an organization implies that users will exchange information and opinions about sales technology, a process that can affect how salespeople feel about technology. Thus, when an adequate number of peers are already using the system, then it is easier for an individual to ask others or get advice about how to use the system and, therefore, to reduce perceived risk and learning time.[181] In other instances, the social pressure that salespeople feel when their colleagues are already utilizing technology can trigger them to adopt the system in order to stay in line with the rest of the sales force.

Two recent studies have shown that when superiors (e.g., sales managers and regional sales managers) use sales technology, salespeople will make more use of the system.[182] This may be the result of persuasive communication mechanisms, which are employed by superiors and which may convey social information that urges salespeople to use the system. In other words, through power and legitimacy mechanisms, leaders' use of sales technologies signals to salespeople that the effort is valued.

Task-technology fit (TTF) has been proposed as an important factor in effective technology implementation.[195] In general, TTF involves the correspondence among task, technology, and user characteristics. In other words, a sales technology that is good for a specific individual will not be equally effective under a different context, such as in a different organizational setting. Consequently, a sales manager's job is to identify salespeople's needs, which should then be matched to the functionalities of the system and the task the salespeople are called on to perform.[196] For instance, a highly complex sales-based CRM system, which offers many capabilities but is rather demanding for an average user, will possibly fail to be integrated into a salesperson's job if no adequate training and support is provided.

Managing an International Sales Technology Implementation

The preceding discussion elaborated on a series of factors that can facilitate smooth system implementation when the organization is operating in a single country. Global firms, however, market their goods and services in multiple countries that may differ substantially in their market, economic, legal, and cultural conditions. As a consequence, global organizations may find it difficult to implement sales technologies across countries using the same process. Unfortunately, the literature on global IT implementation is sparse, at best. Thus, this section aims at elaborating on the difficulties and challenges that global sales organizations face during a sales technology implementation and offering specific guidelines to executives charged with such a difficult task. Specifically, we identify four challenges related to a global sales technology implementation.

The *first challenge* deals with the availability of the same software or application suite across all countries in which the organization operates.

Global firms usually desire to implement the same software in all of their subsidiaries to allow for centralized control over the sales technology initiative and secure efficiency gains in terms of implementation and support costs. In some instances, however, the company adopts a sales technology solution that is provided by a vendor that markets its products only to a portion of the countries the buying organization operates. This, however, creates the dilemma of whether it is wise to adopt the particular sales technology solution in some countries and adopt another solution for the rest of the countries. This is so because different solutions and applications may lead to confusion and incompatibility matters. But even when a sales technology vendor operates in all countries, it might be difficult or cost-ineffective to select the same system across all countries. This might be because vendors do not provide their services across all countries, and adopting organizations will thus have to select more than one vendor to maintain an adequate level of service. For instance, an American vendor that provides excellent service in the United Kingdom may not be able to provide the same level of service and technical support for its client's subsidiary in Spain. There are many factors that prevent vendors from a standardized presence across countries, the most important being the international strategy they adopt in different countries. The American vendor, for example, may decide to follow a direct export model in the United Kingdom by establishing a subsidiary, while it may decide to operate in Spain through a value-added reseller or an independent agent. These two strategies have different implications for a global organization that wants to implement software in the aforementioned two countries. The level of service, as well as employee knowledge and involvement, will not be the same between the United Kingdom and Spain, thereby creating problems for the adopting organization. Finally, sales technology vendors may not maintain the same market presence across all countries in which an organization operates its subsidiaries. Consider, for instance, a European sales technology vendor that has limited or weak presence in the United States. A French multinational company interested in implementing a system in its U.S. subsidiary may have to select a U.S.-based vendor to implement the system.

The *second challenge* global organizations are facing deals with the omnipresent dilemma of deciding whether to buy or make the sales technology. In many instances, organizations decide to outsource the development of the sales technology to an organization that manufactures and markets sales technology solutions. In such a case, the sales technology solution is outsourced to an "out-house" vendor. In other instances, however, organizations decide to develop their own sales technology, often termed as an "in-house" solution. The decision as to what option should be preferred is contingent on many factors, the most prominent being the cost effectiveness associated with developing an "in-house" versus an "out-house" system. A second factor that must be taken into consideration pertains to the level of expertise and skill that the company possesses regarding the development of sales technologies. Finally, a third factor that a global organization must weigh when making such decisions revolves around the ability of the company to feed the system with the appropriate data needed for the system to operate. In particular, one of the main reasons that companies decide to outsource the development of a sales technology is that global vendors may provide companies with data that make the sales technology fully operational and useful.

The *third challenge* is related to cultural differences that exist across countries, which may have an important influence on technology acceptance.[197] Though there are several cultural dimensions in which countries may differ, four of the most common dimensions include[198] (a) power distance, (b) uncertainty avoidance, (c) individualism versus collectivism, and (d) masculinity versus femininity.

Power distance refers to the extent to which members of a culture accept equal distribution of power and hierarchical structures. In countries scoring relatively high on power distance (e.g., France) the implementation process may take more time when compared to countries with relatively lower levels of power distance (e.g., the United States). This is so because managers in high power-distance contexts cannot cut corners to save time but rather must follow strict interpersonal interactions with lower-level employees as well as a top-down hierarchical approach.[199] Moreover, in countries where power distance is valued more, employees may be more inclined to use an IT since usage can give them more power and thus get them closer to upper management.[200]

Countries also differ with respect to how they deal with ambiguity and uncertainty (i.e., uncertainty avoidance dimension). Thus, in countries scoring relatively high in uncertainty avoidance (e.g. Japan), implementation must follow a planned process with little deviation in order for fear of the unknown to be alleviated, thus making introduction of the technology more welcomed among employees. However, such a process can increase the amount of time needed for effective implementation.

Collectivism, which pertains to the importance of the group in contrast to an individual, may also impact on the implementation process. In countries scoring relatively high on collectivism (e.g., Asian countries), salespeople will be reluctant not to use the IT when their colleagues are already using it. For instance, one study shows that subjective norms (i.e., others' influence on one's behavior) influence behavioral intention to use IT in China, but not in the United States,[201] which is a relatively individualistic country. This result might be an outcome of collectivism inherent in the Chinese culture, where the norms of the group and the society convey social meanings that can have a strong impact on individual behavior.

Likewise, how high or low a country scores on masculinity may exert influence on sales technology implementation. In relatively highly masculine cultures (e.g., Mexico), in which people focus on strength, success, and confidence, peer and supervisor pressure to use sales technology may be less important than in highly feminine cultures (e.g., Denmark).

A final cultural influence, which is not related to the aforementioned four dimensions, refers to general predispositions and attitudes toward technology as a function of a national culture. Salespeople working in the United States, for instance, may have a more positive attitude toward technology than salespeople, say, working in South Africa. Not paying attention to such culture-related differences may often lead to different success rates of technological systems across different countries in which a global organization operates. In particular, there may be important differences in how easily or how quickly a sales technology is accepted and used by salespeople working in different countries. Or, it may be the case that different cultures value different antecedents to acceptance. For instance, one meta-analytic study found that "in western cultures, perceived usefulness seems to be more important in determining intentions and actual use, while ease of use is key in non-Western cultures."[202] In another study, it was shown that both perceived usefulness and ease of use are instrumental in explaining intentions to accept technology in the United States but not in China.[203] Differences as to how much interpersonal interaction among employees is valued across countries may also account for the different acceptance rates.

Finally, a *fourth challenge* for global sales organizations is related to issues of data protection and privacy across countries. Data protection varies greatly among countries and can quickly turn out to be a real nightmare for organizations trying to manage a global sales technology implementation effort. The most profound differences are between members of the European Union (EU) and other countries such as the United States, Japan, China, and Canada.[204] For instance, in many EU countries, legislation prevents pharmaceutical firms from gathering and analyzing data about individual physicians' prescription behavior. However, this is not the case in the United States. With the assumption that data constitute an integral part of a sales technology, it is apparent how difficult it is for global firms to follow the same model of implementation across countries.

Summary

Effective implementation of a sales technology should be viewed as a planned process that is affected by several factors. Specifically, these factors can be organized around four interrelated themes: (a) system characteristics, (b) individual differences, (c) organizational influences, and (d) environmental influences. Managers aiming at implementing a sales technology into their organization must take all of these factors into account. Beyond these factors, however, there are four additional challenges that managers may confront in their effort to effectively implement a sales technology across countries.

CHAPTER 4

Performance Implications of Sales Technology

Chapter Overview

In the preceding chapters, we covered how a sales organization can facilitate the process of effective implementation by stimulating users to adopt and start using the sales technology. Of course, having users accept and use the technology is of great importance, but what happens after salespeople have started using it? After all, sales technology implementation is ultimately aimed at increasing sales force performance. Thus, it is natural for someone to ask, In what way(s) does sales technology impact on salesperson performance and to what extent? These fundamental issues, which are related to technology implementation, constitute the focus of the chapter.

We begin by briefly elaborating on the so-called IT-productivity paradox, which occurs at the firm level. Next, we proceed with a detailed discussion regarding the impact of information technology (IT) on individual-level performance that includes a presentation of a fundamental framework in IT research, namely the DeLone and McLean model, which describes how IT impacts individual performance. To facilitate understanding of how IT impacts salesperson performance, we make a distinction between salesperson productivity, efficiency, and effectiveness. Finally, we conclude by distilling the extant literature and presenting a blueprint that maps the various pathways through which technology usage influences salesperson performance.

Information Technology-Productivity Paradox

Researchers across subareas of management science have been systematically investigating the relationship between investments in IT and firm performance for the past 40 years.[1] In spite of the impressive research effort in this area, the evidence is inconclusive. In particular, while a set of studies shows that the relationship is positive,[2] a second set shows that the relationship is either nonsignificant or negative.[3] These conflicting results have become known as the "Information Technology-Productivity Paradox," which occurs at the firm level of analysis. Thus, while most would agree that IT usage allows a firm to achieve high work quality in less time and with less effort, its influence on a firm's financial performance is not so apparent.

A multitude of explanations has been offered, each one aspiring to shed light on the IT-productivity paradox. Perhaps the best treatise on the subject has been offered by Brynjolfsson and Yang in their exhaustive review of the relevant literature.[4] The authors state that there are four basic explanations for the paradoxical nature of the IT-performance relationship:

1. Mismeasurement of outputs and inputs
2. Lags due to learning and adjustment
3. Redistribution and dissipation of profits
4. Mismanagement of information and technology

The first two explanations refer to weaknesses in the methods employed for measuring and modeling the parameters of the problem. Specifically, the first explanation states that while IT exerts a positive influence on performance, bad measurement prohibits researchers from specifying the true relationship. Indeed, the authors argue that measurement fallacies constitute the single biggest problem in crystallizing our understanding of the IT-performance relationship.[5]

In the second explanation, the introduction of a new IT usually presupposes that users will need some time to learn and adapt to the new work reality; thus, if a long period of time intervenes between investment in IT and performance payoffs, as it is the case with technologies that aim to develop a sustainable competitive advantage, then it might be very difficult to measure the impact of IT on performance by using short-term-oriented performance measures.

The latter two explanations constitute an entirely different perspective in that they assume that IT is not actually related to performance. Specifically, the third explanation argues that not all users will benefit the same from using a specific IT but rather that only some will enjoy performance improvements, possibly at the expense of the rest. However, this explanation refers to a nation's economy level rather than to the level of the firm.

Finally, the fourth explanation deals with the managerial processes and corrective actions employed by organizations implementing IT. Specifically, many firms implement IT at the wrong time, use the wrong process, do not provide the necessary support, and do not reengineer business processes immediately affected by IT.

Besides these four general explanations, however, a myriad of others has been offered in the extant literature with the aim of providing a more veridical picture of the IT-productivity paradox. Specifically, some authors have underlined that it is impossible to measure performance improvements without taking a contingency or contextual approach to IT implementation that allows for an explicit consideration of factors related to the organization and its environment.[6] These factors may exert a moderating effect on the relationship between IT and performance such that the relationship is positive only under certain conditions.[7] For instance, one study found that IT investment is positively related to profits and sales when companies are operating in markets characterized by high environmental dynamism or when companies follow a product diversification strategy.[8] In the same vein, a second study found that IT usage by sales managers improves performance only when the environment is highly uncertain or competitive,[9] whereas a third study found that only larger firms enjoy performance improvements from IT.[10] Yet, the contingency approach has not received support across all circumstances, as evidenced in one study that found that firm strategy, type, and size do not moderate the IT-performance relationship.[11]

Another possible explanation of the IT-productivity paradox refers to what has been termed as the "strategic necessity hypothesis," which states that an IT will enhance firm performance only when IT is not directly available to rival firms.[12] Clearly, making such an assumption in the context of sales technology implementation is not realistic, given that sales technologies are either commercially available or can be developed by almost any company in a given industry.

According to other researchers, there may be two additional reasons for the IT-productivity paradox.[13] First, the strategic value of IT varies across sectors of economic activity.[14] Second, they point out that it is particularly difficult to isolate the effects of IT from other factors.

Relatively recently, it has been proposed that the traditional metrics of productivity have to be reconsidered.[15] In other words, the impact of IT on performance should not be solely measured on the basis of financial metrics such as profits, revenues, or any other financial dimension of firm performance. In addition, employing the level of IT investment is not an adequate index of IT performance, since converting the initial investment to effective system implementation constitutes a problem on its own.[16] As an example, consider a firm spending large amounts of money implementing IT applications without, however, securing that the applications are effectively integrated into organizational processes or that the applications are used by the intended users.[17] As such, proponents of this perspective suggest that any effort to specify the relationship between IT and performance should incorporate both tangible and intangible dimensions of performance.[18] This set of authors disagrees with prior work on the existence of an IT-productivity paradox since they believe that IT does exert an impact on performance, but that it does so through more intangible and less quantifiable aspects of performance. Such intangible aspects of performance may include, among others, the creation of competitive advantage, an increase in speed and responsiveness, job enrichment, quality improvement, improvement of customer relations and customer service, securement of future transactions, increase in interorganizational trust, and enhancement of team spirit and company image. Consequently, IT improves firm performance, but it does so in an indirect and more complex manner than initially hypothesized.[19]

The rationale for an indirect influence on performance is as follows. IT influences fundamental processes that are responsible for generating value, as well as administrative processes, including information management, control, coordination, and communication processes.[20] For instance, IT may help firms to conduct existing activities more efficiently but also to conduct entirely new activities that were not possible with older technology, such as being more responsive to customers' needs, more flexible, and more coordinated.[21] It is through such processes that IT comes to have an effect on a firm's financial performance, which renders performance assessment a tough task, since it is rather hard to quantify such intangible benefits stemming from IT investments.

Given the aforementioned limitations of the more "traditional" metrics for assessing the impact of IT, some authors have argued that the intensity or degree of IT usage constitutes a better index for assessing the performance implications of IT than the level of IT investment.[22] In particular, it has been proposed that the degree of IT usage is the basic variable through which IT impacts performance, since usage represents a necessary, though not sufficient, condition for valuating the impact of IT on firm performance.[23] Additionally, the degree of usage has practical utility for managers, given that it can be directly controlled, fixed, and fine-tuned.

We do have to note, however, that employing usage as a proxy for IT impact has its own limitations. First, users may not be willing or able to indicate their real level of usage,[24] and second, some authors cast doubts on whether increased levels of usage will necessarily lead to enhanced performance, especially when usage is not voluntarily.[25]

The aforementioned discussion leads us to conclude that the IT-performance paradox can be attributed not to a single factor but rather to a complex array of factors.[26] This acknowledgment sets the stage for a better understanding of the relationship between sales technology usage and performance, which constitutes the goal of the next section.

The Impact of Information Technology on Individual-Level Performance

The DeLone and McLean Model (D&MM)

Perhaps no other model of information system (IS) success than that presented by DeLone and McLean[27] has received such a great degree of attention in the academic literature. By reviewing and synthesizing a vast number of prior studies, the authors developed a framework, namely, the DeLone and McLean model (D&MM), for predicting IS success (see Table 4.1). In particular, the model proposes that an IS influences individual and organizational performance primarily through two important mediating variables: (a) use and (b) user satisfaction.

Use refers to "consumption of an IS or its output described in terms of actual or self-reported usage," whereas user satisfaction is defined as the "approval or likability of an IS and its output."[28] In turn, use and user satisfaction are both affected by the quality of both the system and the information it generates. System quality refers to "the desired characteristics of the information system itself who produces the information," such as perceived usefulness, convenience, ease of use, portability, functionality, ease of learning, and ability to be integrated with other systems. Information quality refers to "the information product for desired characteristics such as accuracy, meaningfulness, and timeliness";[29] other proxies for information quality might be report reliability, clarity, completeness, and relevance.

Essentially, the D&MM advocates that for a system to positively impact on performance, it has to be used by individuals who must also feel satisfied with its use. If the system is not used by individuals, it cannot generate any benefits. Though use is a necessary condition for influencing performance, however, this does not mean that it is also a sufficient one;[30] indeed, individuals may extensively use the system but in the wrong way, a situation that does not allow for performance improvements. Thus, for firms to reap benefits from system implementation, they have to make sure that the system is used in a consistent and well manner.[31] Nevertheless, the results of two recent meta-analyses suggest that to engage in effective and satisfied system usage, employees should perceive that the system and the information it produces is of high quality.[32]

Quite recently, the D&MM has been revised and updated[33] (see Table 4.2). In this newer version, the authors have made two major changes. First, they add two new constructs, namely, "intentions to use" and

Table 4.1. DeLone and McLean Model of Information System Success (D&MM)

Predictors	Mediators	Outcome(s)
• System quality	• Use	• Individual impact
• Information quality	• User satisfaction	• Organizational impact

Table 4.2. Updated DeLone and McLean Model of Information System Success

Predictors	Mediators	Outcome(s)
• System quality	• Intention to use	• Net benefits
• Information quality	• Use	
• Service quality	• User satisfaction	

"service quality." Second, they group individual and organizational impact measures into a single impact category called "net benefits." "Intentions to use" refers to "expected future consumption of an IS or its output";[34] "service quality" represents the "support of users by the IS department, often measured by the responsiveness, reliability, and empathy of the support organization";[35] and "net benefits" refers to "the effect an IS has on an individual, group, organization, industry, society, etc., which is often measured in terms of organizational performance, perceived usefulness, and affect on work practices."[36]

Since its introduction, the D&MM has been applied, extended, and subjected to empirical scrutiny across a wide range of research settings and contexts.[37] For instance, one study found that user satisfaction is strongly related to user performance,[38] whereas a second study provides evidence that user satisfaction and usage are related to individual performance, though usage mediates the relationship between user satisfaction and performance.[39] In a similar vein, a third study tested the relationships between user satisfaction, usage, and individual performance to find that while user satisfaction is significantly (and positively) related to performance, usage is not.[40] Recently, an attempt has been made to unify the technology acceptance model and the D&MM in a sales force context.[41] The authors make a distinction between user satisfaction with timeliness of data and user satisfaction with system's operations and capabilities to find that it is through perceived usefulness—rather than through user satisfaction and acceptance—that sales-based customer relationship management (CRM) systems impact salesperson performance.

Notwithstanding these conflicting findings, a recent meta-analysis provides strong evidence in favor of the model relationships.[42] In particular, the results of the meta-analysis suggest that both use and user satisfaction result in positive performance improvements, albeit user satisfaction appears to be far more important in explaining net benefits when compared to use.

Salesperson Productivity, Efficiency, and Effectiveness

Before proceeding with a discussion of how sales technology might influence salesperson performance, it is important to make a distinction between three often-confused terms: "salesperson productivity," "salesperson efficiency," and "salesperson effectiveness." This distinction is useful for understanding the performance implications of sales technology.

Efficiency refers to efforts for minimizing inputs, maximizing outputs, or both.[43] Accordingly, sales efficiency seeks to achieve "more-for-less," such as increasing sales force outcomes while decreasing sales force costs.[44] Effectiveness refers to "the distance between observed outputs and a set of desired goals,"[45] or the efforts to increase the accomplishment of sales force objectives, such as increasing sales revenues or market share.[46] The prolific Peter Drucker offers another perspective on the difference between efficiency and effectiveness: "Efficiency in concerned with doing things right. Effectiveness is doing the right things."[47]

Apparently, a salesperson can be effective (i.e., achieving objectives) but not necessarily efficient (i.e., spending too much) and vice versa. This view is consistent with Sheth and Sisodia's[48] definition of marketing productivity, which is conceptualized as "the quantifiable value added by the marketing function, relative to its costs," and is viewed as comprising the dimensions of both effectiveness and efficiency. To be productive, therefore, a salesperson has to be effectively efficient or achieve objectives while making efficient use of resources.

On the basis of this discussion, it is apparent that best-performing companies aim at increasing sales force productivity by meeting both efficiency and effectiveness objectives when implementing sales technology. To illustrate why this is the case, consider the following four scenarios. Based on combinations of efficiency and effectiveness, a sales technology can help salespeople be

1. both effective and efficient,
2. effective but not efficient,
3. efficient but not effective,
4. neither efficient nor effective.

Clearly, the first scenario represents companies that get the most out of their sales technology investment, since salespeople increase both sides of the profit equation (i.e., costs and revenues). In contrast, the last scenario represents the least desired situation, since salespeople are facing many troubles with achieving desired outcomes in an efficient manner. The second and third scenarios represent trade-offs, where companies are able to realize either high sales force efficiency or effectiveness, while not being able to meet the other objective.

The Impact of Sales Technology on Salesperson Performance

Advances in information technologies, such as sales-based CRM and sales force automation (SFA) systems, offer new capabilities that promise to enhance both the sales force's productivity and the sales management's decision-making quality, accuracy, and speed. According to a large number of academic and business articles,[49] these improvements are realized in a variety of ways, such as the following:

1. Freeing up sales force time from administrative work
2. Allowing for the effective management of more information (information efficiency and synergy)
3. Streamlining the sales process and reducing sales cycle
4. Allowing for better contact and call planning
5. Increasing efficiency and effectiveness
6. Allowing for better management of sales expenses
7. Allowing for faster and more effective lead-conversion processes
8. Enhancing inter- and intracompany communication
9. Improving customer relations and satisfaction
10. Enhancing reporting mechanisms
11. Improving sales force morale, image, and professionalism
12. Facilitating coordination and control
13. Enhancing market learning/knowledge/innovation

Reality, however, may be different. According to a recent survey,[50] only 4% of firms can claim that their CRM systems are very successful and deliver all benefits, whereas proverbial reports of failure statistics show that CRM failure rates can range from 18% to 75%.[51] Given this hard reality, it is not surprising that several studies have been conducted to investigate whether these claims are realized in practice. Table 4.3 provides a summary of these studies, with the aim of facilitating understanding regarding the impact of sales technology on salespeople.

Consistent with what has been advocated in the extant literature,[52] we make a distinction between tangible and intangible benefits of sales technology, as presented in Table 4.3. This represents an important distinction, given that the benefits of computerization may manifest in less tangible areas of performance improvement. Specifically, tangible benefits refer to easily quantifiable productivity gains, which can come in the form of streamlining cash flows, reducing sales expenses, and increasing top-line revenues. Intangible benefits are not easily quantifiable gains, such as improved work quality, enhanced communication, deeper customer-needs understanding, and increased sales force morale.[53]

A careful inspection of Table 4.3 reveals at least five major implications for the effective management of sales technology implementation. First, the majority of studies that have been conducted to date show that sales technology is significantly and positively related to tangible benefits such as sales force productivity (i.e., efficiency and effectiveness). In addition, the findings from two studies suggest that productivity can be either enhanced or decreased depending on the type of use.[54] However, a small number of studies provide evidence of either a negative or a nonsignificant relationship.

Second, it is notable, according to one study, that the relationship between usage and performance is curvilinear in that technology may be detrimental to productivity at very high or very low levels of usage;[55] this finding corroborates the suggestion made by Sundaram and his colleagues[56] for effectively, rather than merely, using technology.

Third, sales technology may not be directly related to sales force productivity; rather, the effects of sales technology are indirect through other variables (i.e., mediating paths). Specifically, a significant number of studies have shown that the impact of technology usage on performance is mediated by variables such as customer service, sales presentation skills, adaptive selling, expended effort, and relationship quality.[57]

Fourth, the influence of sales technology on sales force productivity may be contingent on the characteristics of the context in which sales technology implementation takes place. The context can refer to characteristics of the technology, the salesperson, the organization, as well as the market. Thus, a number of studies have advanced knowledge by showing that variables such as user support, training, empowering leadership, and a salesperson's past performance can moderate the usage-performance relationship.[58]

Fifth, sales technology is related not only to tangible outcomes but also to intangible ones, such as improved communication, ability to access information, morale, and image.[59]

Drawing on the distilled knowledge presented in Table 4.3, we develop a conceptual framework mapping the mediational pathways of sales technology's influences on sales force productivity (see Figure 4.1). As shown in Figure 4.1, utilization of sales technology results in increases in sales force tangible and intangible benefits, both of which positively impact sales force productivity through two pathways: first, by stimulating positive customer reactions (e.g., loyalty and satisfaction), and second, by optimally allocating expensive sales resources (i.e., time, budget, and number/duration/frequency of sales calls) across tiers of customers. This conceptualization draws heavily from prior work suggesting that a firm's marketing actions improve performance through customer satisfaction and loyalty and through optimal resource allocation, which refers to the process of directing resources toward the right customer at the right time and with the right cost.[60] In other words, the framework represents a "blueprint" depicting the chain of influences from technology utilization to sales force productivity through "mediating pathways."

The blueprint has important ramifications for managers charged with sales technology implementation in their organizations. First, rather than hypothesizing that using technology will directly influence salesperson performance, managers should map the sales activities that will be impacted by technology introduction. For instance, managers need to specify which aspects of the selling process (e.g., customer targeting, sales presentation, customer needs understanding, etc.) will be impacted by technology and in what way.

Second, understanding the specific influences on sales process implies that managers develop a set of key performance indicators (KPIs) that allow monitoring and tracking of performance improvements (see chapter 5).

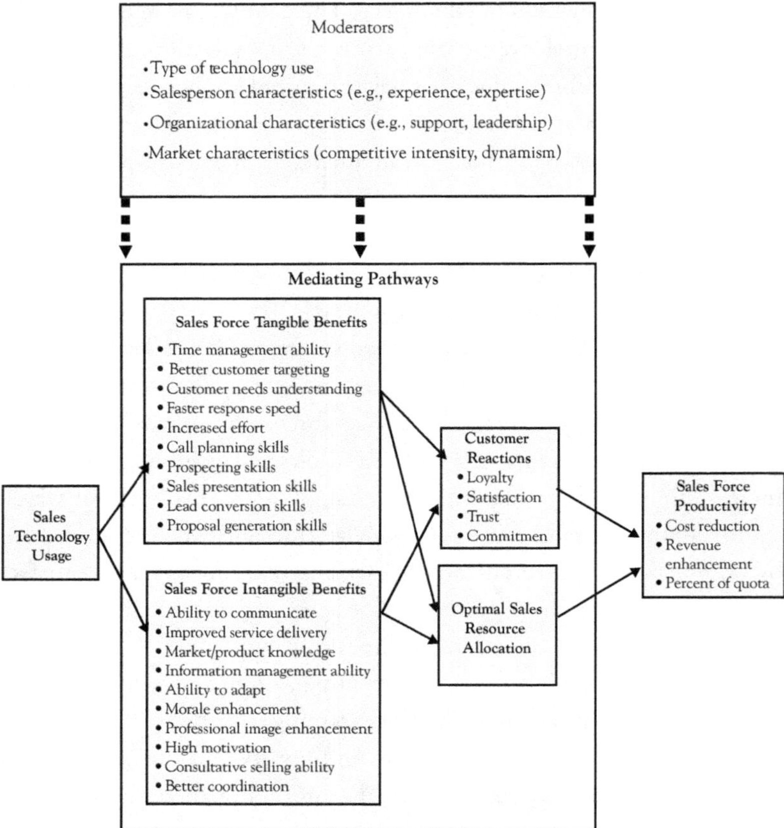

Figure 4.1. A blueprint mapping the pathways of sales technology's influences on sales force productivity.

Third, increases in sales force productivity may be realized after a considerable period of time and in the form of either positive customer reactions or optimal sales resource allocation. For example, consider a salesperson that has integrated sales technology into her current job practices. She is able to retrieve relevant information regarding the most profitable customers in her territory, and thus improve her ability to alter call patterns, targeting approaches, and sales messages to fit the importance of each customer. As such, she might increase her ability to allocate resources in a wiser manner, and thereby achieve higher cost efficiencies. Further, she may also use the technology to improve her knowledge regarding customers' needs, service them better, and, as such, increase customer satisfaction and share of wallet, which represents one indicator of customer loyalty. As a consequence, she might get more sales revenue from her customers that will improve her overall productivity in the long run.

Fourth, managers need to pay attention to the specific context of implementation, such as the characteristics of the sales force, the organization, and the market, all of which may exert a moderating influence (i.e., alter the impact) in the relationship between technology usage and sales force productivity. For example, experienced or less productive salespeople may get less in terms of productivity improvement from using the system compared to inexperienced or more productive salespeople. Likewise, using the system to enhance the understanding of customer needs might generate more benefits for salespeople operating under conditions of high competitive intensity compared to salespeople operating in less "hostile" markets.

Summary

This chapter presented a detailed analysis of how and to what extent sales technologies might impact on salesperson productivity. Specifically, we reviewed the relevant literature on the IT-productivity paradox and then we presented the seminal model of IT success, namely, the DeLone and McLean model. We concluded that to realize performance improvements from a sales technology implementation, managers must ensure that the system will be accepted and eventually used by individual salespeople. We then elaborated on the notion of salesperson productivity, which is a function of salesperson effectiveness and efficiency. This was followed by a comprehensive review of the studies examining the link between sales technology use and salesperson productivity. On the basis of this review, we developed a blueprint that maps the mediating pathways from technology use to salesperson productivity. The blueprint should serve as a useful device for managers charged with assessing the impact of sales technology on sales force performance.

Table 4.3. Benefits of Sales Technology for the Sales Force: Review of the Empirical Literature

Studies (in alphabetical order)	Benefits	
	Tangible benefits: Productivity	Intangible benefits
Ahearne, Hughes, and Schillewaert (2007)	Percentage of quota (+ through call productivity, sales presentation skills, targeting skills, and knowledge)	
Ahearne, Jelinek, and Rapp (2005)	Effectiveness: percent-to-quota (+ under adequate user support and training) Efficiency: average number of sales calls per day (+ under adequate user support)	
Ahearne, Jones, Rapp, and Mathieu (2008)	Percentage of quota (+ through adaptability and customer service)	
Ahearne, Srinivasan, and Weinstein (2004)	Percentage of quota (+ up to an optimum point)	
Avlonitis and Panagopoulos (2005)	Effectiveness (ns)	
Brewer (1999)	Sales per customer (+) New customers (+)	
Buehrer, Senecal, and Pullins (2005)	Productivity (+)	Communication with customers (+)
Bush, Bush, Orr, and Rocco (2007)	Efficiency (+) Effectiveness (-)	

Table 4.3. Benefits of Sales Technology for the Sales Force: Review of the Empirical Literature (cont.)

Studies (in alphabetical order)	Benefits	
	Tangible benefits: Productivity	Intangible benefits
Cronin and Davenport (1990)	Time management (+) Order processing (+)	Communication (+) Knowledge management (+) Image (+) Sales culture (+)
Engle and Barnes (2000)	Percentage of sales quota (+)	
Erffmeyer and Johnson (2001)	Efficiency (+) Revenue generation (+)	Communication (+) Access to information (+) Customer access to information (+)
Fram and McCarthy (2000)	Time spent with customers (+)	
Hunter and Perreault (2006)	Internal role performance (+) Performance with customers (+ through information effectiveness and smart selling behaviors—that is, planning and adaptive selling)	
Hunter and Perreault (2007)	Relationship building performance (+ through relationship-forging tasks when using sales technology to analyze/communicate information) Internal administrative performance (– when using sales technology to analyze information) Internal administrative performance (+ when using sales technology to access information)	

Table 4.3. Benefits of Sales Technology for the Sales Force: Review of the Empirical Literature (cont.)

Studies (in alphabetical order)	Benefits	
	Tangible benefits: Productivity	Intangible benefits
Keillor, Bashaw, and Pettijohn (1997)	Sales revenues (+) Productivity (+)	
Ko and Dennis (2004)	Percentage of sales quota (+) Percentage of sales quota (+ for high-performing sales reps)	
Lapierre and Denier (2005)		Communication effectiveness (+) Communication effectiveness (+ under higher organizational change processes, managerial empowerment and innovative/ supportive organizational culture)
Mathieu, Ahearne, and Taylor (2007)	Percentage of quota (+) Percentage of quota (+ under more empowering leadership)	

Table 4.3. Benefits of Sales Technology for the Sales Force: Review of the Empirical Literature (cont.)

Studies (in alphabetical order)	Benefits	
	Tangible benefits: Productivity	Intangible benefits
Moncrief, Lamb, and Mackay (1991)	Profits (+) Productivity (+) Efficiency (+) Time spent on administrative tasks (-) Sales force complaints (-) Paperwork (-) Customer complaints (-) Time spent with customers (ns) No. of sales calls (ns) Sales expenses (-)	Morale (+) Decision-making effectiveness (+) Complexity of sales job (+)
Moutot and Bascoul (2008)	Sales call effectiveness (+ or – depending on the type of SFA use) Sales call efficiency (+ or – depending on the type of SFA use) Proposal generation effectiveness (+, ns, or – depending on the type of SFA use) Proposal generation efficiency (+ or – depending on the type of SFA use) Reporting effectiveness (+ or ns depending on the type of SFA use) Reporting efficiency (+ and ns depending on the type of SFA use)	

Table 4.3. Benefits of Sales Technology for the Sales Force: Review of the Empirical Literature (cont.)

Studies (in alphabetical order)	Benefits	
	Tangible benefits: Productivity	Intangible benefits
Park, Kim, Dubinsky, and Lee (in press)	Effectiveness (+ through market information processing, adaptive selling behaviors, and relationship quality)	
Pullig, Maxham, and Hair (2002)	Account prospecting (+) Account development (+) Creation of buyer profiles (+)	
Rapp, Agnihotri, and Forbes (2008)	Percentage of quota (+ through effort when using SFA) Percentage of quota (+ through adaptive selling when using CRM)	
Rivers and Dart (1999)	Savings (ns) Efficiency (ns)	
Robinson, Marshall, and Stamps (2005)	Job performance (+ through adaptive selling)	
Senecal, Pullins, and Buehrer (2007)	Effectiveness (ns)	
Speier and Venkatesh (2002)	Number of contracts (+ through job and professional fit) Sales volume (+ through job and professional fit)	
Stoddard, Clopton, and Avila (2002)	Productivity (+) Sales costs (ns)	Teamwork (+) Communication (+)

Table 4.3. Benefits of Sales Technology for the Sales Force: Review of the Empirical Literature (cont.)

Studies (in alphabetical order)	Benefits	
	Tangible benefits: Productivity	Intangible benefits
Sundaram, Schwarz, Jones, and Chin (2007)	Productivity (+)	
Taylor (1993a)	Productivity (+) Sales expenses (-)	
Yoo, Schuler, and Sneide (2003)	Annual dollar sales volume (mostly ns) Annual number of transactions (mostly ns) Annual personal income (mostly ns)	

Note: (+), (-), and (ns) denote a positive, negative, and nonsignificant relationship between technology usage and the focal benefit, respectively.

CHAPTER 5

Measuring the Impact of Sales Technologies

Chapter Overview

No matter how sophisticated a sales technology is and how ready the company is for accepting the change associated with technology introduction, managers need to define and articulate the business case of the technology. Doing so, however, implies that firms develop quantifiable metrics to gauge and track the success of system implementation.[1] Consequently, the present chapter deals with how managers can develop a set of key performance indicators (KPIs) that can serve as a performance monitoring apparatus during sales technology implementation. To this end, we provide a wide array of different KPIs that can fit into any implementation context and any type of technology. Finally, the chapter concludes by presenting a financial-based valuation method that can be employed to assess the return on sales technology investment (ROSTI).

Developing Key Performance Indicators (KPIs)

As mentioned before, companies implement sales technologies with the aim of enhancing communication with customers, increasing selling time, allocating sales resources in a more efficient manner, and having faster access to relevant and timely information. Through such gains, companies expect to increase salesperson performance, enhance customer satisfaction, and leverage customer relationships. In spite of the anecdotal evidence suggesting positive returns on customer relationship management (CRM) investment, however, academic research pinpoints that the outcomes of sales technology are manifested through a complex network of effects that may involve trade-offs.[2] That said, companies implementing sales technologies should strive to develop the appropriate metrics and KPIs on which they can assess the effectiveness and efficiency gains from CRM systems.[3] This is imperative since an absence of systematic and quality measurement of the implementation process prevents firms from knowing whether they have achieved their implementation objectives. Unfortunately, as revealed by recent studies, only 30% to 50% of companies reported that they regularly use metrics to measure how CRM systems are performing.[4]

Perhaps one of the key reasons for why companies are not engaged in measuring the success of their sales technologies is precisely the lack of a common definition regarding what constitutes the success of an implementation effort. The work of Klein and Sorra[5] is particularly illuminating in this regard. Specifically, the effectiveness of an innovation (e.g., sales technology) refers to the "benefits an organization receives as a result of its implementation of a given innovation."[6] As reviewed in chapter 4, one of the key measures of implementation success is achieving the intended level of usage of an information technology (IT). However, gaining the committed use of a technology by individual users is a necessary, but not sufficient, condition for technology's effectiveness. In other words, salespeople must use sales technologies frequently in order to gain enhanced performance, though it is not certain that increased use will eventually lead to performance improvement.[7]

Against this paucity of a set of commonly accepted metrics, we next present a host of KPIs that can be employed by adopting organizations to track and monitor implementation progress (see Table 5.1). These KPIs constitute a comprehensive set in that their inception is based on both market research reports and academic studies.[8] In developing the KPIs, we employ the nomenclature of the six categories of information system (IS) success metrics that has been put forward by DeLone and Mclean.[9] Accordingly, we group the KPIs into six key areas:

1. System quality
2. Information quality
3. Service quality
4. Use
5. User satisfaction
6. Net benefits

Table 5.1. A Dashboard of KPIs for Assessing Sales Technology Implementation Success

System quality	Use
• Number of user complaints that the system is not useful	• Total time of use
• Frequency of user complaints that the system is not useful	• Adoption rate = 100 × (number of users fully using the system/total number of targeted users)
• Number of user complaints that the system is difficult to use	• Duration of active use = number of active minutes per day or active hours per week
• Frequency of user complaints that the system is difficult to use	• Duration of inactivity = number of inactive minutes per day or inactive hours per week
• Number of user complaints that users are not confident in using the system	• Duration of connect time
• Frequency of user complaints that users are not confident in using the system	• Number of different functions/modules used
• Number of user complaints related to difficulty in learning the system	• Duration of using a specific function/module
• Frequency of user complaints related to difficulty in learning the system	• Frequency of using a specific function/module
• Number of user complaints that the system cannot be customized to meet specific needs	• Recency of using a specific function/module
• Frequency of user complaints that the system cannot be customized to meet specific needs	• Number of screens used
• Number of user complaints that the system cannot be integrated with other systems	• Duration of screen usage
• Frequency of user complaints that the system cannot be integrated with other systems	• Frequency of screen usage
	• Recency of using a specific screen
	• Number of orders processed
	• Frequency of processing orders
	• Recency of last processed order
	• Number of requests/queries for specific information
	• Frequency of requesting/querying specific information

*Table 5.1. A Dashboard of KPIs for Assessing Sales Technology
Implementation Success (cont.)*

System quality	Use
	• Recency of requesting/querying specific information
	• Number of proposals generated using the system
	• Frequency of using the system to generate proposals
	• Recency of using the system to generate proposals
	• Number of data records accessed
	• Frequency of accessing data records
	• Recency of accessing data records
	• Number of data records modified
	• Frequency of modifying data records
	• Recency of modifying data records
	• Number of information exchanges with peers
	• Frequency of exchanging information with peers
	• Recency of exchanging information with peers
	• Number of messages sent to customers
	• Number of messages sent to management
	• Frequency of sending messages to customers
	• Frequency of sending messages to management
	• Recency of sending messages to customers
	• Recency of sending messages to management
	• Number of uploads/downloads
	• Frequency of uploads/downloads
	• Recency of uploads/downloads
	• Number of sales call reports generated
	• Frequency of generating sales call reports
	• Recency of generating sales call reports

Table 5.1. A Dashboard of KPIs for Assessing Sales Technology Implementation Success (cont.)

System quality	Use
	• Number of sales expense reports generated
	• Frequency of generating sales expense reports
	• Recency of generating sales expense reports
	• Number of log-ins
	• Frequency of log-ins
	• Recency of log-ins
	• Percentage (%) of work time that the system is used
	• Percentage (%) of nonwork time that the system is used
	• Navigation patterns

Information quality	User satisfaction
• Number of complaints referring to inaccurate information	• Index measuring user satisfaction with the system
• Frequency of complaints referring to inaccurate information	• Index measuring user satisfaction with the information
• Number of complaints referring to irrelevant information	• Index measuring user satisfaction with support services
• Frequency of complaints referring to irrelevant information	
• Number of complaints referring to incomplete information	
• Frequency of complaints referring to incomplete information	
• Number of complaints referring to ambiguous information	
• Frequency of complaints referring to ambiguous information	
• Number of complaints referring to outdated information	
• Frequency of complaints referring to outdated information	
• Number of complaints referring to information overload	

Table 5.1. A Dashboard of KPIs for Assessing Sales Technology Implementation Success (cont.)

Information quality	User satisfaction
• Frequency of complaints referring to information overload	
Service quality	**Net benefits**
• Number of complaints referring to IT employees being unreliable	• Percentage (%) of reports completed on time
• Frequency of complaints referring to IT employees being unreliable	• Percentage (%) of reports completed accurately
• Number of complaints referring to IT employees being unresponsive to users' requests	• Number of errors in reporting
• Frequency of complaints referring to IT employees being unresponsive to users' requests	• Frequency of errors in reporting
• Number of complaints referring to IT personnel lacking needed knowledge	• Recency of errors in reporting
• Frequency of complaints referring to IT personnel lacking needed knowledge	• Time spent on nonselling/administrative activities
• Average time taken to resolve user complaints	• Time spent in the field
• Average number of queries handled	• Time needed to draft a sales proposal
• Average number of technical support requests	• Time needed to generate a lead
• Number of connectivity "blackouts"	• Time needed to qualify a lead into a prospect
• Frequency of connectivity "blackouts"	• Time needed to convert a prospect into a customer
• Duration of connectivity "blackouts"	• Time needed for a new rep to reach "full productivity"
• Number of server "downtime"	• Time needed to complete order processing
• Frequency of server "downtime"	• Time needed to complete reporting
• Duration of server "downtime"	• Number of customer support queries resolved
	• Number of leads generated
	• Number of prospects qualified
	• Number of proposals generated
	• Lead conversion ratio
	• Number of closed sales per number of sales calls

Table 5.1. A Dashboard of KPIs for Assessing Sales Technology Implementation Success (cont.)

Service quality	Net benefits
	• Number of sales calls
	• Duration of sales calls
	• Frequency of sales calls
	• Percentage (%) of sales quotas achieved
	• Number of professional social network contacts
	• Number of rebates/discounts
	• Percentage (%) increase in margins
	• Percentage (%) increase in revenues
	• Sales revenues
	• Revenue growth
	• Amount of sales expenses per sales call
	• Amount of sales revenues per sales call
	• Amount of sales expenses per closed sale
	• Cost to convert a lead into a prospect
	• Degree of product knowledge
	• Degree of market knowledge
	• Percentage (%) of realized sales forecasts
	• Number of new (organic) customers obtained
	• Number of new customers stolen from competition
	• Number of customers retained
	• Number of lost customers recaptured
	• Number of defected customers
	• Average customer satisfaction
	• Average customer lifetime value
	• Average customer profitability
	• Number of referrals generated by customers
	• Average customer share of wallet
	• Average customer size of wallet
	• Average number of products sold to a customer (cross-selling)
	• Average number of upgrades/add-ons of the product sold to a customer (up-selling)

Collectively, the six key areas and their associated KPIs compose a "dashboard" that brings the key sales technology implementation metrics into a single display.[10] Each area of KPIs can be used to monitor implementation success and indicate specific areas where corrective actions might be pursued to smooth the adoption rate. Consider, for instance, a firm that receives an inordinate number of complaints regarding the quality of information that the system provides to its users. Such a situation might signal that the system presents problems with information accuracy, completeness, and relevance that kept salespeople from trusting the system and, therefore, from using it. Thus, management might need to conduct a detailed analysis in order to determine the exact nature of the problem and then proceed by crafting an improvement plan (e.g., a change in customer data collection processes).

There are three main ways that the KPIs displayed in Table 5.1 can be deployed. First, the KPIs can be used either as stand-alone measures or in combination. Utilizing stand-alone metrics is particularly useful for conducting an in-depth diagnosis of specific areas that need improvement, whereas combining metrics is useful for understanding relationships between metrics. For instance, by testing whether there is a significant relationship between the duration of active use and the time needed to qualify a lead into a prospect, management can have an early understanding of whether certain aspects of technology usage are related to salesperson performance and, subsequently, what aspects of usage salespeople need to focus their attention on in order to improve performance. Second, KPIs can be used as snap shots to monitor progress at a particular point in time or at different points in time (e.g., daily, weekly, or monthly) to track behaviors and activities longitudinally. Third, KPIs can be calculated at the individual salesperson level or at any other aggregated level, such as the sales team, district, region, division, or the entire sales organization.

It is appropriate to inject three notes of caution at this point. First, echoing the sentiment by DeLone and McLean,[11] we must stress that there is no universally accepted metric or set of metrics that can measure a sales technology's success; rather, the choice of metrics should be guided by a careful assessment of the technology being implemented, the context under investigation (e.g., voluntarily vs. mandatory use), as well as the specific objectives of the assessment procedure. For instance, managers need to answer questions such as, for what purpose is the assessment done, or what kind of information do we really need to improve implementation? Thus, rather than blindly employing the metrics listed in Table 5.1, executives need to judiciously decide which ones suit their context and adjust them to the company's specific needs.

Second, modern CRM systems offer a wide range of KPIs that can be employed to track almost any kind of sales force behavior related to technology usage. That said, however, managers need to be aware that more is not better when evaluating technology implementation—they have to carefully select those metrics that really fit into the situation and that can help them derive better decisions. After all, what is the purpose of spending time on developing, measuring, and reading KPIs that will not assist management in making better decisions?

Finally, the temptation to track and monitor every aspect of usage behavior in order to fix suboptimal utilization should be balanced against salespeople's privacy rights. As Ahearne and colleagues note,[12] an open policy of tracking usage might result in dysfunctional consequences, such as decreased feelings of trust due to micromanagement and usage manipulation to accord with management directives. For example, it is not uncommon to observe salespeople leaving the system open for hours in order to manipulate tracking mechanisms without, however, using the system at all; of course, the development of appropriate KPIs can catch such manipulative behaviors by measuring inactivity rather than duration, for instance. Nevertheless, selecting KPIs for tracking usage patterns should always be weighed against the monitoring policy that the organization is pursuing.

Calculating the Return on Sales Technology Investment (ROSTI)

Overview of the ROSTI Method

Every firm implementing a sales technology, such as a sales-based CRM system, desires to know whether the investment made was worth its money. In other instances, management may be in need of a yardstick that allows for the comparison between alternative solutions provided by different vendors before the firm makes a selection. In any case, assessing the return of an IT investment appears to be an imperative, since an IT solution can cost an inordinate amount of money for adopting firms, especially larger ones that deploy the system to several hundreds of users across business units and countries. In fact, there is evidence suggesting that CRM systems may cost from $60 million to $130 million in total,[13] or from $5,000 to $18,000 per user per year.[14] Given these figures, the total cost for equipping a sales force of, say, 100 people can range from $500,000 to $1,800,000. With such high expenditures, a natural question for managers to ask is, what is the return of such an investment, or is the CRM contributing to profit improvements? Consistent with the IT-productivity paradox discussed previously, the evidence from recent empirical studies, which have attempted to provide an answer to questions like those raised here, is rather inconclusive. For instance, one study pinpoints that CRM technology use is indirectly associated with organizational performance through marketing capabilities;[15] a second study shows that while CRM implementation hurts cost efficiencies, because it requires substantial investments, it nevertheless enhances a firm's ability to earn profits by generating revenues that exceed the additional costs associated with CRM implementation;[16] yet a third study concludes that CRM investments are not associated with stock returns or profitability.[17] Given the importance of assessing the profit impact of an IT, we next turn our attention at delineating how management can valuate returns from investment in sales technologies.

One should bear in mind, however, that quantifying the impact of IT investment in the sales organization is always a challenging procedure. This is largely due to the fact that many of the accrued benefits from IT implementation are intangible, such as strategic advantages, improved decision making, and so forth.[18] Thus, many executives have found, over the years, that the assessment of an IT's performance impact can quickly turn out to be a chase for the holy grail. Even with these well-known problems, however, it is management's job to pursue a detailed evaluation of the outcomes of the IT initiative using one of available capital budgeting methods, such as the return on investment (ROI), the internal rate of return, the net present value, and the economic value-added method. Given its preponderance in C-level decision-making contexts, as well as its parsimonious nature, our focus here is on the ROI. However, the logic presented herein can be extended to other valuation methods.

Broadly speaking, ROI represents what a firm gets in return for what it gives to a specific investment, commonly expressed as a percentage. Beyond this general definition, however, there are many variations of the basic ROI formula, such as those defining ROI as the discounted accumulated net benefits stemming from a particular investment over a certain time period and divided by initial costs. It is this latter definition to which we focus our attention, since it can give executives a more complete picture than the basic definition. Support for this choice comes from two facts. First, Rust and colleagues suggest, "The correct usage of ROI measures in marketing requires an analysis of future cash flows."[19] Second, the definition of ROI adopted here takes into account the time value of money that represents an important aspect of decision-making efforts to justify investments. Regardless of the definition employed, however, ROI can be employed to compare alternative investments. For instance, a company can calculate the ROI for different sales force automation (SFA) and CRM solutions, which can be subsequently incorporated into a "vendor scorecard" that is used to aid selection among different solutions. By adjusting the basic tenets of the theory underlying the ROI concept[20] to the context of sales technology investments, one can calculate the ROSTI using the formula displayed in Figure 5.1.

As seen in Figure 5.1, the formula for calculating ROSTI consists of five components, which are subsequently discussed:

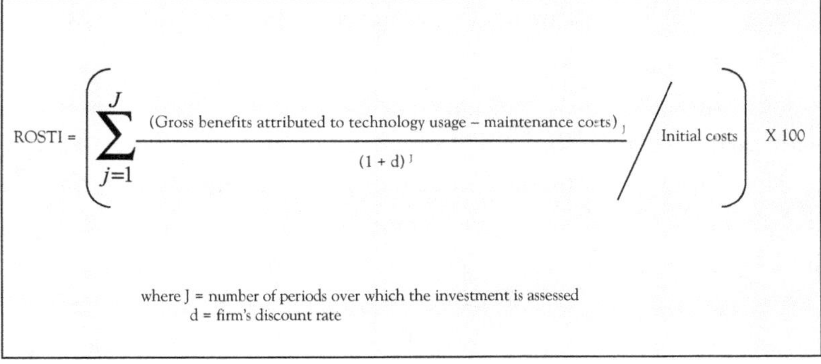

Figure 5.1. An approach for calculating the return on sales technology investment (ROSTI).

1. The gross benefits stemming from technology usage
2. The initial costs associated with the technology investment
3. The costs to maintain the system
4. The discount rate
5. The time period over which ROI is measured

The first component refers to the gross benefits that can be attributed to system usage. As was shown in chapter 4, sales technology can improve sales force productivity. The main sources of benefits come from enhancing either of the following two key areas: (a) sales force effectiveness (e.g., achieve a higher percentage of sales quotas) and (b) sales force efficiency (e.g., decrease customer acquisition and retention costs or produce more in less time). Ideally, a sales technology can enhance sales force productivity by decreasing the time salespeople need to accomplish administrative tasks (e.g., reporting, managing contacts, etc.), thereby freeing up time for making more calls to customers. Sidebar 5.1 details a relatively straightforward method that can be utilized by managers aiming to assess the gross benefits stemming from sales-force productivity improvements due to investments in a specific technology. Using the same logic presented herein, a company can develop realistic scenarios for calculating any additional benefit that it expects the technology to contribute, either in the form of achieving a higher percentage of sales objectives achieved (i.e., sales force effectiveness) or streamlining the costs of operating the sales organization (i.e., sales efficiency). For instance, a company can use the method to calculate the increase in profit margins either because of the enhanced ability to identify and target more profitable accounts or because of the decrease in customer acquisition and retention costs.

The method displayed in Sidebar 5.1 is very useful prior to sales technology adoption, when the company evaluates the benefits associated with each potential solution. In other instances, however, the technology has already been implemented and users have already begun to use the technology. Thus, companies may employ a more complex, and presumably more precise, method that is based on a statistical tool called "regression analysis" to nail down the benefits associated with technology implementation. The method, developed by Engle and Barnes[21] and presented in Sidebar 5.2, consists of several steps. The method can be conducted either by administering a short survey to users after some time

> ## Sidebar 5.1. A General Method for Estimating Gross Benefits Stemming from Sales Technology Usage
>
> **Consider, for instance, a sales organization that employs 100 salespeople. The organization expects that the sales force can decrease time spent on administrative work by 1 hour per day due to the introduction of a sales technology.**
>
> **A decrease by 1 hour per day allows salespeople to complete one additional sales call to a new customer per working day.**
>
> **Assuming that salespeople work 240 days per year, the sales technology allows the sales force to do 240 more sales calls per year per rep or 24,000 additional calls per year for the entire sales force.**
>
> **If the firm knows from past records that 5% of calls made to new customers are eventually converted to closed sales and the average order size is $1,000, then the sales technology can help the company to make an additional $1,200,000 (or 5% × 24,000 × $1,000) per year.**
>
> **Therefore, in monetary terms, investing in the specific sales technology might help the company to earn an annual gross benefit of more than $1 million.**

of initial adoption or by monitoring and recording actual usage behavior. The analysis of the data can be subsequently conducted by means of a standard statistical package.

The second and third components of the ROSTI formula deal with the costs associated with the sales technology investment. Generally speaking, one can distinguish between two categories of costs: (a) initial costs, or the portion of costs that represents any one-time costs incurred in implementing the system, and (b) maintenance costs, or any recurring costs that exist along the entire lifetime of the technology. Table 5.2 lists some of the most frequently encountered costs associated with each of the two categories. The list of costs can be used as a useful guide for executives charged with the difficult task of identifying the costs associated with sales technology investments. As seen in Table 5.2, both initial and maintenance costs include expenses items related to software, hardware,

Sidebar 5.2. The Engle and Barnes Method for Estimating Gross Benefits Stemming from Sales Technology Usage

The method consists of a series of steps that managers must follow:

1. Identification of all relevant sales force activities that are affected by sales technology usage (e.g., call planning, customer targeting, contact management, making sales presentations, etc.).

2. Estimation of the extent to which salespeople perform each of the aforementioned activities by using the sales technology.

   Estimation can be based on archival data (e.g., actual recorded usage) or by running a short survey among salespeople using a 5-point scale, where "1 = I don't use the technology at all to conduct this activity" and "5 = I use the technology to the greatest possible extent to conduct this activity."

3. Estimation of the percentage (%) of revenues that is attributed to system usage.

   One way of doing this is to estimate a multiple regression model with salesperson performance (e.g., percentage of quota) as the dependent variable and the extent of performing each sales force activity as independent variables. The r-squared (%) generated by the regression equation is the targeted estimation. For instance, an r-squared of 14% means that 14% of the variance in salesperson performance is attributed to system usage.

4. Sorting salespeople according to their performance (e.g., percentage of sales quotas achieved).

5. Grouping salespeople into two groups: top performers and low performers.

   For instance, top performers are those who stand at one standard deviation above mean performance; low performers

are those who stand at one standard deviation below mean performance.

    If the number of salespeople is adequately large, say more than 100 salespeople, one can distinguish between three groups for better precision. This can be done by breaking down the sales force on the basis of a quartile split, and taking the upper quartile (top 33% of cases) and lower quartile (lower 33% of cases), while excluding the median quartile.

6. **Calculation of the difference between the average monetary amount of sales revenues produced by top performers and that produced by low performers.**

7. **Multiplication of the r-squared (%) calculated in Step 3 with the difference in the monetary amount of sales revenues calculated in Step 6. The outcome of this multiplication represents the monetary amount of sales attributed to the usage of the sales technology per salesperson.**

8. **Multiply the outcome of Step 7 with the number of salespeople in the company. The result is the monetary amount of sales attributed to sales technology usage for the entire sales force.**

and service purchases. It is noteworthy that software and hardware costs can account up to 50% of total costs.[22] One should note, however, that the final decision as to which of these cost items should be included in ROSTI calculation depends on the specific context under investigation, since different companies have different cost structures and employ different methods for calculating IT-related costs.

Calculating ROSTI also calls for deciding on the discount rate that is going to be employed. The discount rate represents a general notion that can be interpreted in a variety of ways, depending on the investment context and the financial assumptions made. Definitions of the discount rate, for instance, range from the weighted average cost of capital for the firm, to the market rate of interest, to the reinvestment rate of the firm. Whatever approach managers take, however, the important thing is to consider how the selected definition of the discount rate impacts the calculation

Table 5.2. List of Initial and Maintenance Cost Items Associated With Sales Technology Investments

Initial costs	Maintenance costs
Application software investments (rent or purchasing fees or in-house development)	Software upgrade fees
Hardware investments (e.g., servers, notebooks, data warehouses, mobile phones)	Software maintenance fees (e.g., bug fixes)
Costs incurring from setup, synchronization, and integration of current IT systems with the new technology	Annual software license fees
Development and merging of databases	Application service provider (ASP) fees
Customization costs	Supporting software upgrade fees
Project management costs	Syndicated data fees
Security costs	Mobile service provider fees
Consulting services costs	Hardware upgrade costs
Costs stemming from recruiting, training, and compensating employees who will manage implementation	Recurring training costs
Business process reengineering (e.g., sales process, customer-targeting process)	Recurring IT support costs
IT support (e.g., help desk)	Recurring project management costs
Initial user training	
Implementation support costs (e.g., roll-out costs, workshop costs, etc.)	Recurring consulting services costs
Other initial costs	Other recurring costs

of ROSTI and, subsequently, the decision-making processes of the firm. Executives charged with the task of calculating ROSTI may find it very beneficial to discuss the firm's current discount rate with a knowledgeable person such as the chief financial officer.

The final component of the ROSTI calculation refers to the time period over which ROI is measured. The decision of the time span for evaluation differs among companies due to different financial resources, objectives, and methods for assessing the performance of capital projects such as a sales technology. Our view is that, under current conditions of the IT market, a company can expect that a specific sales technology becomes obsolete after a period of around 3 years. This view is reinforced by evidence from academic and business studies, which show that the average payback period can range from a minimum of 12 months to a maximum of 3 years.[23] As such, we will use this time period for the numerical example presented subsequently. When making a decision regarding the time period that will be employed in the calculation of ROSTI, however, managers are encouraged to consult the opinions of both IT and finance personnel who are very knowledgeable about current company practices, trends in the IT market, and past returns from IT investments.

An Illustrative Example of ROSTI Calculation

In order to aid managers in gaining a deeper understanding of how they can employ the ROSTI formula to assess the financial return on sales technology investment, we now present a numerical example of a company that has decided to implement a sales-based CRM system. We make the assumption that the discount rate (d) for the company is 0.10 (or 10%) and that the time span (J) of the investment is 3 years. The initial costs—including software, hardware, consulting, project management, and other expenses—average $250,137, whereas the maintenance costs are fixed to the amount of $52,800 annually. In addition, the company estimates that technology usage will contribute a gross benefit of $500,000, $600,000, and $750,000 to the sales organization for each of the 3 years, respectively. The company expects these benefits primarily due to enhancements in sales force productivity and based on prior experience with an old IT system. In addition, the company makes the assumption that the gross benefit increases over time to reflect the theory-based scenario that the technology will become more effective as users gain experience and as the system is infused into salespeople's work practices. Table 5.3 exhibits how executives can use the aforementioned pieces of information to calculate ROSTI by employing the formula presented in Figure 5.1.

Table 5.3. A Numerical Example of ROSTI Calculation

Components of ROSTI	Year 1	Year 2	Year 3
1. Estimated gross benefit	$500,000	$600,000	$750,000
2. Maintenance costs	$52,800	$52,800	$52,800
3. Net benefits: (1) – (2)	$447,200	$547,200	$697,200
4. Discounted factor: $(1 + d)^j$	$(1+0.10)^1$	$(1+0.10)^2$	$(1+0.10)^3$
5. Discounted net benefits: (3) / (4)	$406,545	$452,231	$523,817
6. Sum of discounted net benefits	$406,545 + $452,231 + $523,817 = $1,382,593		
7. Initial costs	$250,137		
8. ROSTI (6) / (7)	5.527 or 552.7%		

The resulting ROSTI of 552.7% shows managers of this company the percentage return they are expected to get over the 3 years of investment. This figure can be either compared to similar figures of competing solutions or as a stand-alone measure to make technology investment decisions.

Summary

One of the most difficult tasks managers face during sales technology implementation is to justify the business case of the associated technology. This entails that management is able to quantify the impact of the technology on the sales organization. Likewise, to ensure the success of the implementation effort, management needs to develop a set of KPIs to allow for the effective monitoring of the entire process. Against these realities, this chapter offers a wide array of different KPIs, which are grouped around six key areas of technology implementation and that can fit into any implementation context. Finally, the chapter concludes by presenting a managerial formula for assessing the return on sales technology investment (ROSTI) as well as a numerical example on how this formula can be employed in practice.

CHAPTER 6

Implementation in Practice

A Road Map to Success

Chapter Overview

As contemplated in the chapters throughout this book, getting the most out of a sales technology implementation requires more than selecting a good solution from a trustful vendor, training users, and then rolling out the technology. It requires careful planning, resource allocation, and effective execution of a series of interrelated activities. Drawing on the insights gained from the detailed review of the academic and business literature presented in chapters 2 and 3, as well as on the author's involvement in sales technology implementation, this last chapter provides executives, researchers, and students with a comprehensive, yet practical, process for implementation that consists of three distinct stages. Each stage is deconstructed to a series of activities that represent the essential work that needs to be carried out in order to effectively and efficiently implement sales technology and to gain returns on investment.

A Three-Stage Process for Effective Sales Technology Implementation

In chapter 2, we presented a generic process (see Figure 2.1) that identifies three distinct stages of sales technology implementation: (a) preadoption, (b) adoption, and (c) postadoption. Based on the identification of these three stages, we next elaborate on the essential work and activities that need to be conducted by executives when implementing a sales technology such as a sales-based customer relationship management (CRM) system. Our focus here is on providing executives with managerially relevant guidelines that can be applied to real life situations. Accordingly,

Figure 6.1 presents a managerial process comprising three distinct stages, each with a different set of goals and the tasks and activities to be accomplished. Before proceeding with discussing the various stages and activities, however, it is felt that some elaboration is needed at this point on three important aspects of the proposed implementation process.

First, sales technology implementation is viewed as a planned process consisting of a series of stages and activities. It is a planned process since executives can plan the execution of each stage beforehand and each stage or activity can, and should, be separately managed.

Second, the stages and activities of the proposed process may not be applicable to all contexts and in the same fashion since, from time to time, executives may deliberately choose to skip activities or even an entire stage due to time pressures. Notwithstanding, however, executives are advised to pay extreme attention to the effective execution of each and every activity before moving on to the next one. This is especially important when the company is doing this for the very first time. Companies need to move step by step to secure that everyone (salespeople, managers, information technology employees, etc.) is in agreement with the outcomes of each activity.

Finally, a common misperception of executives is that they have to completely eliminate every barrier that the company faces during system implementation. Driven by their commitment to perfection, they tend to forget that no company effort is ever perfect. Though chasing perfection is a legitimate activity, managers often realize that they have to compromise their initial aspirations. Some barriers are "time proof" and they are never eliminated so long as the same people and organizational processes are in place. As such, the chase to overcome all barriers can quickly exhaust users' patience and consume precious time and resources. Instead, the real gain comes from trying to implement the stages and their associated activities in the most realistic manner that fits best with the company's unique idiosyncrasies.

The Preadoption Stage

The preadoption stage deals with organizational-level activities aimed at analyzing a firm's current situation and planning and preparing for the implementation process. At this stage, an executive or a team of executives

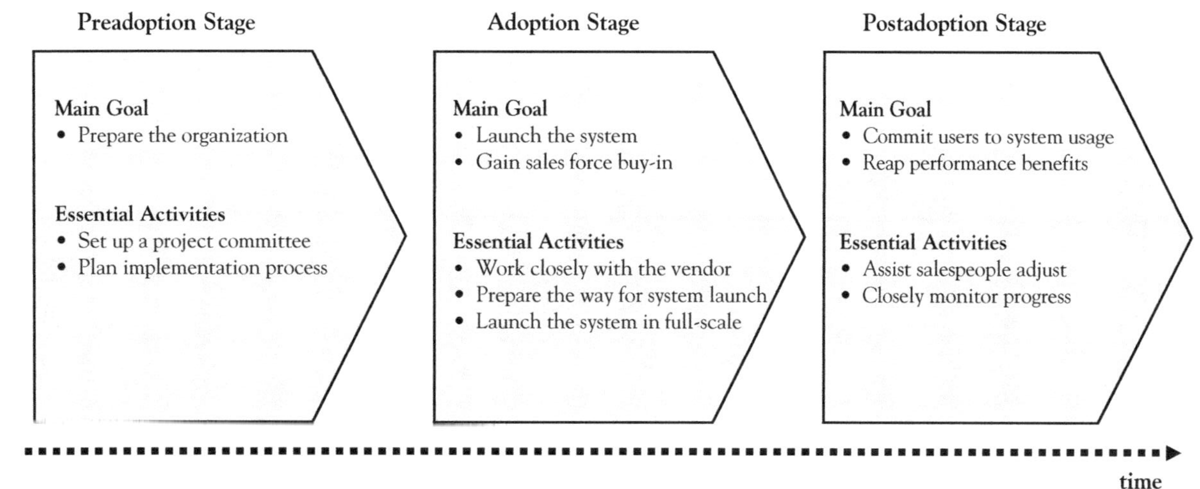

Figure 6.1. A three-stage process for effective sales technology implementation.

usually become aware of the organization's need to implement a sales technology. These individuals then initiate the implementation process by setting objectives and planning what is needed before the organization buys and adopts the technology. In what follows, we elaborate on the various activities and essential work that firms need to conduct in order to carry out this stage.

Activity 1: Set Up a Devoted Project Committee

The project committee consists of a team of executives and employees that takes charge of, and leads, the implementation effort. Though variation exists among different companies regarding the roles and responsibilities of the committee, some of the most important activities include specifying company needs, selecting a vendor, working with the vendor to customize the system to the needs of the company, reengineering organizational process, and specifying the types of data that need to be fed into the system.

There are five prerequisites for developing a successful committee. First, the top management of the organization (e.g., CEO) must take an active role up front in the process in order to signal the urgency of the project. If this is not the case, users may perceive that the implementation effort does not represent an important company activity. Of course, top management's involvement should not be a one-time event after which the CEO becomes invisible. To obtain users' buy-in, management has to be systematically engaged in all critical stages of the implementation process.

Second, people comprising the committee must represent all functions of the organization, with strong emphasis on representation of those that are directly impacted by the introduction of the technology. Since sales technologies largely involve the front-office processes of the organization, representation from marketing, sales, service, and operations is critical. Specific attention should be paid to involving executives from both sales and marketing, given that these two functions often have conflicting goals and varied informational needs, which can harm the implementation process if not reconciled early in the process. However, executives from finance, accounting, and other functional areas should have a voice in the committee in order for the project to gain company-wide commitment. Financial executives can also prove to be particularly useful in the process of justifying the financial benefits of the system. In general, the extent to which the company has achieved coordination, information exchange, and structural links among different functional units can play an important role in successful implementation.

Third, the committee should be comprised of people with expertise in technology project management. Ideally, people from information technology (IT) or equivalent functions, where available, possess a great degree of knowledge and expertise regarding the use of technologies and should be involved in the process. Knowing that IT employees are appointed to support system implementation triggers mechanisms of psychological safety. This is so because users and executives feel that someone who is knowledgeable is there for them should the need arise. If the company lacks the necessary talent or IT employees are overloaded in current assignments, a decision must be made at this stage concerning whether to hire external IT consultants to help the organization achieve its objectives.

Fourth, in setting up the project committee, management must clearly articulate the roles and responsibilities of each and every one comprising the committee. This is very important given that employees charged with implementation represent different functions and often work in parallel levels of the organizational hierarchy, thereby increasing chances of confusion regarding who is responsible for what activity and who has the authority to delegate or make decisions. A related problem comes from the fact that employees may lack the time or commitment to the project, since all too often, current appraisal procedures are not adjusted to take into account the new responsibilities. As such, management must ensure that existing goal-setting, evaluation, and rewarding systems change to incorporate the new tasks that employees have to perform as members of the project committee. Otherwise, employees may hesitate to invest time or resources in the project. Sidebar 6.1 illustrates an example of such an undesirable situation.

Sidebar 6.1. An Illustrative Example of Implementation Failure in a Large Mobile-Services Provider

A large multinational mobile-services provider failed to successfully implement a CRM system when the chief information officer (CIO) declined to commit IT resources to develop the new customer database architecture.

The task of developing the new architecture, which was going to feed the system, was so demanding in terms of resource commitment that it quickly became cost-ineffective for the IT department. Indeed, the objective was to enable management to develop key performance indicators (KPIs) at the level of individual customers. With a multimillion-subscriber base, however, the task required time commitments from a number of IT employees.

The reason for resistance by the CIO was simple: the IT department was operating as an independent cost-profit center; thus, committing resources to the project would have decreased departmental profitability and productivity. As a consequence, the project was stalled for several months before the board of directors decided to change the current evaluation and rewarding mechanisms.

Finally, making the leader of the project committee accountable for the whole process is imperative. The person who is held accountable must be chosen very carefully on the basis of prior experience, expertise, and competencies in managing large-scale projects. Among other things, the leader's job consists of setting usage objectives, monitoring usage and outcomes associated with implementation, and developing KPIs to justify the investment. All too often, however, responsibility for implementation is hastily delegated to individuals who are not held responsible for the outcomes. In addition to the project leader, for companies with multiple business units or subsidiaries across countries, an executive should be held responsible for supervising implementation at each business unit or subsidiary. In conclusion, management needs to clearly identify exactly who is taking charge of the effort and who is held accountable for the success or failure of the implementation effort.

Activity 2: Plan the Implementation Process

The next activity during the first stage is to get the project committee to plan the implementation process. In so doing, the committee needs to make a number of important decisions, which are subsequently discussed.

1. Set objectives related to sales technology implementation. The committee has to set the objectives of technology implementation early in the process. Specifically, the committee has to make it crystal clear exactly what is expected from system implementation, how the system will help the company in meeting its marketing objectives, and how the system will facilitate sales processes. Consistent with any other objective setting procedure, however, goals should be specific, measurable, achievable, realistic, and time specific. Objective setting is an important managerial device that is used for controlling, motivating, and directing employees' efforts. As such, the selection of specific objectives should always be linked to the firm's ability to reliably measure user performance against these objectives. Managers should note that there is no universally accepted set of goals that can be applied to all firms—even among firms in the same industry. Instead, different firms have different strategic priorities and needs, and, as such, goals should also reflect these differences.[1] For instance, some firms will focus on reducing nonselling time, increasing sales force productivity, and decreasing costs; some will set goals for increasing customer satisfaction ratings or system usage; and some will want to facilitate resource allocation, reporting mechanisms, and budgeting decisions. Though it is tempting to set a wide array of objectives, it is wiser and more realistic to focus on a limited number of objectives that the company can actually work toward meeting.

When setting goals for the implementation effort, managers need to consider the type of sales force compensation plan. Consider, for instance, the case where management sets the objective of developing better reporting mechanisms through system utilization. It will be very challenging to persuade salespeople working on a straight commission plan to use the system for reporting purposes, since they have very little interaction with the company and are usually working with minimal or no supervision at all. As such, any planned effort to change their work practices can stumble at the sales force's resistance to change.

2. Set up a clear customer strategy. Generally speaking, a customer strategy refers to organizational processes and decisions for allocating resources in order to manage customer relationships. Specifically, these processes refer to how customers are identified, attracted, grown, and maintained. Setting up a customer strategy at the level of the sales function involves outlining the processes for (a) acquiring new customers (e.g., lead generation and prospecting), (b) retaining and growing existing customer bases (e.g., through cross-selling and up-selling), (c) recapturing lost customers, and (d) ending relationships with nonprofitable customers. Thus, management has to define and outline the specific tasks and activities that relate to each of the four customer-strategy processes as well as to link each process with the use of the sales technology. For instance, the committee has to explicitly outline how the new sales technology will affect sales processes such as customer targeting, customer analytics, account management, call scheduling, and contact management. In doing so, it is important to focus on sales processes that either need improvement or are just too important for the specific company. Furthermore, one should keep in mind that simply automating sales processes or redesigning the processes to fit into the new reality cannot alone improve performance. The project committee needs to cautiously spell out how the system being implemented will connect to, and impact, customer strategy and customer-linking sales processes that the firm pursues. For instance, executives need to answer questions such as, in what way would we like the system to impact on our sales force's capability of relating and building relationships with customers? Will the system be visible to customers? Do we want it to be? How will the system impact on the functioning of the entire sales organization? Successfully answering such questions, however, implies a deep understanding of how the firm generates value for both itself and its customers.

3. Assess the impact of implementation on users. In successfully planning for implementation, the committee needs to conduct a detailed assessment of the impact of implementation on users. This process includes the following tasks.

First, the company must decide on the type and number of employees to be targeted as potential users of the new technology. A sales technology is usually targeted not only at different customer contact positions but also at different levels in the hierarchy of the organization, such as salespeople, field sales supervisors, and sales managers. Different positions, however, entail different needs.

Second, project leaders need to conduct a detailed assessment of the needs of users who are going to be affected by the sales technology. Perhaps of utmost importance in this regard is that firms need to take into account users' prior experience with sales technologies. Clearly, firms differ in their level of readiness to accept new systems since some have already been using quite advanced systems (e.g., wireless sales force automation solutions) for some time, while others are just beginners in the world of sales technology. Regardless of the experience level of a firm, effective implementation starts with understanding and defining the needs of the people who will be most affected by sales technology implementation. Specifically, the committee needs to collect feedback from employees working from the front lines (i.e., salespeople and marketing employees), who will ultimately be called to integrate the technology in their jobs.[2] Developing a segmentation scheme may prove very useful when implementing a sales technology. Especially in larger organizations (i.e., those employing more than, say, 100 front-line employees), users are never homogeneous in their needs or their reactions toward technology and its impact on their jobs. Management can divide the user population into one or two different segments that can be targeted in different manners. For instance, the committee should consider how to manage implementation among older—and usually technophobic—salespeople who lack the necessary knowledge and skills in using advanced technology, and how to manage younger, newly recruited salespeople. In general, the project committee has to identify any potential negative emotions toward technology, such as fears stemming from anticipation of losing power, autonomy, or one's job, and work toward alleviating those fears on a one-to-one basis. The committee might administer a short survey among targeted users that can be used to uncover their attitudes, fears, and expectations from technology usage. In sum, executives should make sure that the needs of employees are identified and that their voices are heard early in the process of implementation. Careful assessment of firm needs can also serve as a "safety valve" against falling prey to fancy software and services that are just not appropriate for the firm.[3]

4. Decide on the scope of the system. One of the most important decisions related to planning sales technology implementation is to decide on the technology's functional architecture within the wider business and IT infrastructure of the company. This involves the making of two decisions by the project committee.

First, the committee has to decide on the right way of migrating and integrating any old system with the new sales technology. In addition, managers need to decide on how other firm-wide systems, such as enterprise resource planning (ERP) systems, are going to be integrated with the new sales technology. Since ERP systems usually refer to back-office applications (e.g., manufacturing, accounting, operations, and finance), managers have to be very careful regarding how they will handle ERP's integration with a front-office application such as a CRM system. Effective implementation requires that both back- and front-office applications are harmonically orchestrated to allow for a smooth flow of data between the two types of systems.

Second, the committee has to specify the system's functionality that is required to facilitate users' tasks. Since different groups of users perform different tasks and have different needs, the system must factor in different uses and functions. For instance, sales managers often use spreadsheets (i.e., Excel) to project sales volume and to analyze sales territories. Thus, the system must enable managers to export data in a spreadsheet for subsequent analysis. Firms that are either unfamiliar with technology or have been experiencing problems with technology in the past should consider adopting a more prudent approach, such as introducing the technological solution in a piecemeal or multiwave fashion. Specifically, they should initially roll out a limited number of the solution's functions to allow users to adjust their practices, and then move on by introducing more functions.[4]

5. Map and evaluate processes for collecting and integrating information. No matter how sophisticated sales technology is, it cannot be useful if the right type of data is not linked to it. Unfortunately, this is something that is often left aside as an activity of subordinate importance, thereby leading to premature implementation failure. As such, the committee has to carefully plan the type and source of data needed to transform the technology into an effective sales planning and decision-making tool. To this end, companies can develop a table that outlines the relationships between the types and sources of data. An example of how such a table looks is shown in Table 6.1.

Table 6.1. Example of Mapping Data Types and Sources

Type of data	Source of data
• Number of sales calls (daily)	• Salespeople
• Customer satisfaction (quarterly)	• Survey conducted by a market research company
• Customer spending in the product category (monthly)	• Syndicated data source • Salespeople
• Number of competitive sales calls (quarterly)	• Survey conducted by a market research company • Salespeople
• Number of prospects (quarterly)	• Syndicated data source • Salespeople

The decision regarding what types of data are needed should be guided by the organization's sales activities and the relative weight each activity has in the organization's strategy. Deciding on the data source, however, can be more complex, since companies may have to purchase the required data from syndicated sources or market research companies. In other instances, companies can find the needed data in current information systems, or they may have to configure a new procedure for collecting the data through available resources. Thus, it is the committee's job to identify the right source of data and what work needs to be done in order to make the data useful.

Sometimes the necessary pieces of information cannot be extracted from current information systems. In such instances, the company may choose to involve the sales force in the process of gathering market intelligence. Doing so, however, may prove a daunting task because salespeople lack the skills for gathering reliable information, as they are paid and motivated to call on customers and achieve quotas rather than to collect intelligence. In addition, any change in their current work practices, such as uploading information on a daily basis, can be viewed as a time-consuming activity. As such, companies should be extremely careful in identifying what pieces of information are really critical for the success of the implementation and should not ask salespeople to collect an inordinate amount of information. Therefore, important decisions must be made at this stage regarding changes in training, motivation, leadership, and compensation systems, which are needed in order to effectively transform salespeople into a firm's "listening posts."

Regardless of the data source, the committee has to set up control mechanisms or filters to secure the accuracy of the data being collected. There is nothing noisier in the implementation process than providing the sales force with incorrect information about customers and competitive products. If salespeople perceive that the information regarding customer addresses, for instance, is wrong, they will not take the system seriously and will turn away from it. Thus, the committee needs to verify whether the quality of data is adequate in helping salespeople and sales managers effectively conduct their job activities.

6. Decide on privacy issues. Privacy issues, which refer to the privacy rights of either the company or its employees, are turning out to be a critical area of concern when implementing a sales technology. Specifically, the project committee has to pay attention to two key issues.

First, though offering unlimited access to any type of information and to any type of user sounds like a desired strategy for facilitating information exchange, the company has to be very cautious with the level of access that it allows. It may have to restrict some users from being able to access specific types of data. Management has to decide on the level of access it will grant to the sales force, for instance, since salespeople can "poach" customer information from the system and then go to work in a competitive firm, taking all the info with them, or they can manipulate information for personal advancement.[5]

Second, managers need to carefully articulate how information regarding customers and salespeople's activities will be recorded and analyzed. "Big brother" perceptions may discourage salespeople from using the sales technology. The European Union Data Protection Act, for instance, is quite strict on such issues. When implementing a solution for global subsidiaries, therefore, companies need to take legislation factors into consideration (see also the section "Managing an International Sales Technology Implementation" in chapter 3). In any case, the committee has to stay in line with current privacy policies that the company pursues.

7. Decide whether use is voluntarily or not. Whereas mandatory usage should be the desired strategy of most managers, it is the circumstances under which implementation is taking place that influences whether usage should be mandated or not. Specifically, if technology is a relatively new phenomenon in the organization or the majority of users do not have extensive experience with technology, then it might be wiser to have some volunteers experiment with the technology before imposing adoption on the entire sales force.[6] That way, users can be given the opportunity to observe others using the system and exchange information with them before they have to adopt it. Of course, when deciding on the preferred strategy of implementation, one needs to take into account the need or felt pressure for quick implementation.

8. Decide on the budget needed for effective implementation. The project committee needs to make a decision regarding the required budget for effectively meeting the goals of implementation. Basically, the committee needs to budget the expenses that will be required for developing or buying the technology and for conducting the various activities needed for managing its implementation across its entire lifetime. One important task at this stage is to make an optimal estimation by accounting for both direct and indirect expenses related to the implementation process, such as hardware, software, application services, consulting services, training and support, and human resources costs that are needed for managing the whole process. The cost items appearing in Table 5.2 can be particularly helpful in this regard.

9. Decide whether to outsource the development, project management, and support of the sales technology. Generally speaking, when firms decide to implement a sales-related IT, they face two options. The first option is to outsource the development of the technology by buying either a widely available commercial package or a customized solution, which is built by an external developer to fit the exact needs of the firm. The second option refers to in-house development, where the firm uses its own resources and skills to develop a custom-made system. Evidence from a number of market research reports shows that contemporary firms rely mostly on the first option,[7] that is, they rely on a commercial package that can be either purchased or rented. Nevertheless, for some firms, in-house development may still be a viable solution that has to be compared against outsourcing. While there are many parameters that should be weighed when choosing one of the two options, there are three parameters that should be considered as the most important for making such a decision.

1. Time needed to develop an in-house versus buying an off-the-shelf system. In most instances, buying a packaged solution will take less time than developing an in-house system, particularly when the firm has no prior experience or when it is difficult to deploy available resources to the development of the system.

2. Associated costs, including manpower, maintenance, service, and opportunity costs. Usually, customizing a packaged solution or developing an in-house system can quickly become very expensive, but that depends on the skills of the organization and the context of use. Also, there may be "hidden costs" stemming from the utilization of employees' time to develop, integrate, and technically support the system. Finally, the firm needs to weigh its ability to maintain, support, and feed the system with relevant data once the system is developed.

3. The needs of the firm. Clearly, there are situations where the needs of the firm are so unique—due to firm or industry idiosyncrasies—that buying a ready-made solution is not a prudent choice since the system must be reconfigured to fit the exact needs of the firm.[8] However, reconfiguring a commercial system may quickly become cost-inefficient or simply turn out to be a daedal journey, where firms are finding themselves struggling to hastily manage an ocean of incompatible software codes. In such instances, internally developing the system may be the only viable solution. Another occasion where an in-house strategy might be preferred is when firms wish to have complete control over the implementation process. It has to be noted, however, that many vendors today offer "vertical industry" applications that can be suited to fit the specific characteristics and singularities of a specific industry. Thus, in the years to come, it is expected that an increasing number of firms will be relying on commercial solutions rather than building their own.

If the decision is to internally develop the system, the committee has to prepare a technical blueprint that specifies the concept and the functions of the desired system. Once agreement is reached regarding the concept, management needs to proceed by developing the prototype, that is, an initial and incomplete version of the final product that can be used for assessing any additional requirements or specifications that have not been considered. The prototype has to be presented to a sample of targeted users and tested for ease of use and usefulness. That way, management can obtain precious feedback on which system functionalities have to be adjusted, fine-tuned, and further customized in order to meet users' needs. Usually, fine-tuning the prototype occurs in an iterative fashion, involving several rounds of testing, adjusting, and retesting, before the final version of the system is accepted by targeted users.

If the decision is made to outsource the sales technology to a vendor, executives should set clear specifications. With so many solutions available today, specifications can be invaluable in guiding the organization through the maze of selecting the right vendor.

A decision should also be made regarding whether to use an implementation consultant who will assist the committee in managing the entire project. Too often, sales technologies disrupt current practices, sales processes, and activities, and create new realities for salespeople that can lead to lower than desired rates of adoption. In addition, pressing demands for integrating the technology with existent IT systems forces executives to redesign business processes. While these matters can be handled by the project committee, it is often advisable to hire an external "expert" who can help to smooth the implementation effort. In most instances, sales force automation (SFA) or CRM vendors offer high-end consulting services to their clients, either with or without additional charges. In other instances, the firm may have to look elsewhere to get expert advice. Choosing among a plethora of consulting agencies can be a daunting task, however. Presumably, the best way to ensure that the right consultant is hired is to do some homework. Executives need to carefully research the market, ask colleagues for feedback, evaluate the success history of consulting agencies, and compare bids. Generally speaking, consultants with proven experience in implementing sales technologies in the industry in which the firm operates, or consultants that have already been involved in implementing the technology that the firm has chosen, should be the best candidates. Of course, the final decision should be weighed against cost and time considerations, especially for smaller firms that cannot afford to pay large amounts of money in hiring a consultancy agency.

Finally, the committee has to decide who will provide technical support to users and in what form. In small to medium companies, justification for the existence of an IT department is often not feasible, and management may rely on external consultants or the technical support provided by the vendor itself. That can be a daunting task, however, since companies have little or no control over an external consultant's activities. Thus, deciding on whether to outsource the support activities should be balanced against control considerations.

10. Select a sales technology vendor. If a decision has been made to buy a commercially available solution, the committee should proceed by selecting the best alternative. Doing so implies that the committee employs a process for gathering information, comparing, and selecting one out of several alternative solutions. We next elaborate on what essential work needs to be done to facilitate decision making.

First, managers need to cautiously gather information regarding possible vendors and the solutions they are offering. This is very important in order to ensure that the optimal decision will be made. There is a large number of information sources that managers can utilize in this regard, such as syndicated sources, academic studies, industry contacts, articles appearing in specialized business press, and, of course, professional social networking sites (e.g., LinkedIn, PartnerUp), which are changing the way professionals are communicating with their peers across industries and countries. Unleashing the power of these information sources, however, requires that managers are able to glean reliable and relevant information out of an ocean of buzz. Also, when collecting information regarding possible vendors, executives need to make sure that they listen to what their salespeople have to say. Salespeople are in close contact with peers from firms both inside and outside their industries. Thus, they often have formed a well-informed opinion on whether solutions implemented in other organizations are really working and what problems salespeople in these organizations might be confronting.

Second, the committee needs to evaluate vendors and their solutions based on the information gathered during the previous step. Use of a scorecard might be very helpful in the evaluation phase. The scorecard depicts the performance of competing solutions relative to a series of standards or KPIs, as well as each KPI's relative importance (weight) to the company implementing the technology. Potential KPIs that can be incorporated in such a scorecard may include, inter alia, prior experience in the industry, ratio of successful implementations, image and reputation, system functionalities, cost, and ability to customize and integrate the system to existing databases and systems. The section entitled "System Characteristics" in chapter 3 offers a detailed treatise on which aspects of an IT are considered important for gaining users' buy-in and could be employed to update the list of vendor evaluation criteria. Nevertheless, it should be noted that the decision regarding which KPIs will be used to evaluate vendors, as well as their relative weights, should be driven by the specific needs of the firm and given its strategic priorities and management admonitions. Table 6.2 provides an example of how a firm can construct a scorecard to compare a short list of three potential vendors.

Besides the commonly employed list of KPIs, such as those listed in Table 6.2, other less quantifiable factors should be taken into account. For instance, smaller companies sometimes find it hard to partner with a well-known large vendor because the vendor may not care the same for this firm as it does for larger customers. If the committee believes that the company does not constitute an important customer for the vendor under consideration, then the committee should consider alternative options, such as buying from another vendor that can meet company expectations. Also, it is sometimes very effective to exploit the opportunity of a free trial before proceeding to a final decision, since this can minimize any perceived risks.[9] A prepurchase trial allows companies to diagnose several important issues, such as whether the system is perceived as being (a) consistent with the sales force's portfolio of tasks, (b) better than current systems, and (c) useful or easy to use. Thus, the committee should also take into account the provision of free trials when making purchase decisions.

Finally, the committee should select the preferred vendor based on the evaluation process previously described. When making the final decision, executives need to pay particular attention to the terms of the contract that they negotiate with the vendor of their choice. Specific issues that should be put under scrutiny include sales and service terms as well as any potential escrows that can be used to protect firms from vendors going bankrupt.[10]

11. Develop a back-up plan. Sales technology implementation is largely dependent on the proper functioning of IT-related activities and infrastructure. Sometimes, technical problems, such as connection "blackouts" of wireless services, server downtime, and incompatible software

Table 6.2. An Example of a Scorecard Used to Evaluate Potential Solutions and Vendors

KPI evaluation		Vendor					
		Technosystems		Integrated Systems, Inc.		Total Solutions	
KPIs	Weight	KPI Score	Score × Weight	KPI Score	Score × Weight	KPI Score	Score × Weight
System's functionality	0.10	3.00	0.30	5.00	0.50	4.00	0.40
System's ease of use	0.20	2.00	0.40	3.00	0.60	4.00	0.80
Service level	0.30	2.00	0.60	4.00	1.20	2.00	0.60
Experience in the industry	0.05	5.00	0.25	1.00	0.05	3.00	0.15
System customization ability	0.10	4.00	0.40	4.00	0.40	5.00	0.50
Data accuracy and richness	0.20	4.00	0.80	2.00	0.40	3.00	0.60
Global presence	0.05	3.00	0.15	4.00	0.20	2.00	0.10
Total KPI Score	1.00		2.90		**3.35**		3.15

Table 6.2. An Example of a Scorecard Used to Evaluate Potential Solutions and Vendors (cont.)

Additional considerations	Technosystems	Integrated Systems, Inc.	Total Solutions
Initial investment cost	$ 10,000,000	$12,500,000	$9,000,000
Negotiable contract	Yes	Yes	No
Total annual cost (manpower & maintenance) per user	$5,000	$5,500	$4,000
Overall evaluation & decision	• Lowest KPI performance • Relative high cost	• Highest KPI performance • Negotiable contract • Most expensive *PREFERRED SOLUTION*	• Good KPI performance • Nonnegotiable contract • Cheapest solution

Note. Vendors are evaluated on a 5-point scale, where 1 = performs poorly on this KPI, and 5 = outstanding performance on this KPI.

code, can create a lot of confusion and disappointment to an otherwise well-planned implementation. As such, the project committee should develop a contingency plan that delineates how the company should react and proceed should such problems occur. In addition, the contingency plan should account for other critical incidents that may occur during implementation, such as sales force resistance, problems with the vendor relationship, and unexpected cutbacks of implementation budgets.

The Adoption Stage

Once the company has selected a solution, it is time to launch the system in the sales organization. During the adoption stage, the committee has to overcome several challenges, the most important being gaining sales force's buy-in and making them use the system. As we saw in chapters 2 and 3, there is a myriad of factors relating to characteristics of the system, the salesperson, the organization, and the environment that collectively impact users' decisions to accept a system or not. It is exactly these hurdles that the project committee needs to overcome in order to effectively accelerate the implementation process. The good news is that most of these hurdles are managerially controllable. To succeed in this effort, the committee must carefully execute a series of activities, which are subsequently described.

Activity 1: Work Closely With the Vendor

For effective implementation to take place, the committee needs to work closely with the preferred vendor. Indeed, the expertise of the vendor can play a significant role in securing that everything is done in the right way and that the company gains the most from the implementation effort. That said, however, it is not uncommon to confront situations in which the management of the adopting company is attributing poor implementation results to the vendor and its solution. While vendors can play their part in implementation failure, in the vast majority of cases, it is the company itself that is to be blamed. The sales technology vendor market is very mature and proficient at this stage of market evolution, and it is rarely the case that vendors lack the necessary resources or knowledge to help their clients make the most of their investments. In contrast, they usually provide a wide array of training, technical support, and consulting services to substantiate and augment their products so that the latter fits into a client's organizational and technological environment. Rather, the most critical role is played by the project committee that is charged with conveying the particular needs of the company to the vendor. Also, regardless of the sophistication level of the technology being adopted, an absence of a clear and strong customer-centric organizational culture, which reflects a deeply held commitment to serve customers and to rearrange cross-functional processes en route to satisfying customer needs, is what will determine success or failure. Quite often, the predominant difficulty during system implementation is related to people and their mind-sets, especially when these people are high in the organizational hierarchy. Having a strong customer-centric culture can secure that the implementation will succeed, even when the selection of a particular vendor turns out to be a bad choice. Put another way, even if the technology is outstanding, implementation will not be successful if the company downplays innovation or does not have a sharp focus on customers' needs. After all, the same technology is virtually available to all companies; not all, however, can claim to be getting returns on IT investment.

Moreover, the committee needs to partner with the vendor in order to effectively customize sales technology to the specific needs of the organization. Customization refers to the process of altering the system's basic philosophy, functionalities, modules, and parameters to fit the adopting firm's unique needs. Also during this step, the committee has to decide on the functions and modules that will be turned on. Customization is fundamentally a cocreation process in that it should involve employees from both the buying and the supplying firms. Specifically, IT employees must work closely with the vendor in coordinating the process of customization, such as integrating existing systems and databases within the new system.[11] However, since the system is actually going to be used by marketing and sales employees, they should be actively involved in the process of parameterizing the solution. It is very important that companies implementing sales technologies turn on the right features that match the needs and expectations of the users.[12] During customization, members of the project committee need to pay particular attention to relevant employees when making the technology as free of effort as it can be. While customizing a sales technology has many benefits, executives need to pay attention to their organization's own limits in order to make sure they do not go too far with customization.[13]

Activity 2: Prepare the Way for System Launch

Having customized the system to company's needs, the time is right for the committee to set the stage for effective system launch. Specifically, the committee needs to conduct a series of activities, which are detailed in what follows.

1. Communicate. Even when firms have carefully planned the implementation process and have chosen or developed the most appropriate system, salespeople may still resist the initiative because they do not realize its value or potential for increasing their own performance. Consequently, communicating the value of the technology to the sales force comes as an imperative at this stage. But what should be included in the message communicated to salespeople who are often technophobic or who view the initiative as an onerous imposition that steals time from making sales calls? There is no universally applied solution; rather, firms need to take into account the specific needs, attitudes, and perceptions of their own salespeople. To do so, executives can utilize the results of the user-needs assessment conducted in the second activity in the preadoption stage. By using these results, firms can alleviate fears stemming from perceptions of micromanagement, isolation, and power or job loss, while simultaneously illustrating concrete ways of how the system can lead to sales efficiency or effectiveness. For instance, firms can demonstrate how the system facilitates salesperson activities, such as managing accounts, screening profitable leads, and tracking competitive actions. In addition, they have to be clear regarding what management expects salespeople to accomplish through using the system, as well as what types of data must be fed into the system and why. The goal is to manage salespeople's expectations and overcome resistance by selling salespeople on the benefits of system usage.

2. Provide training. As discussed in chapter 3, training is an important determinant of effective implementation in that it can drive users to adopt or reject the system early in the process. Technology-illiterate salespeople usually feel that they are not capable of dealing with the complexities of a new system and are thus inclined to not make use of the system. In other instances, salespeople may feel that they are uncertain or face conflicting demands concerning system usage. As such, training interventions should target increasing feelings of self-efficacy as well as clearly setting out what users are expected to do with the system.

3. Adjust or change sales management systems and practices. Due to the availability of technology, traditional sales management systems and practices may be severely affected. Ideal candidates for transformation are the sales process, organizational structure, reporting mechanisms, communicating norms, meeting arrangements, training, evaluation procedures, and rewarding schemes. For instance, salesperson performance evaluation may change due to an increased availability of data regarding expenses at the individual customer level. Thus, a sales manager's job is to anticipate or assess the degree to which the sales technology will impact the salesperson's activities and to adjust accordingly.

4. Gain field sales supervisors' buy-in of technology. Field sales supervisors have a key role in the implementation process since they are directly responsible for managing, coaching, and leading field salespeople. As such, they have direct influence on their subordinates' behaviors and attitudes. Accordingly, their support of the sales technology might stimulate usage among salespeople. The challenge, therefore, is to involve field sales supervisors in the implementation process as early as possible.

5. Small-scale launch. Prior to rolling out the system in full scale, companies are advised to pilot test it for a short period of time (e.g., 3 months) and to a limited number of users. The objective is to identify any possible problems associated with its usage and to suggest any improvements or adjustments. The committee should target the implementation process toward technology advocates. Ideal candidates for targeting are individuals with a highly innovative profile that have a positive predisposition toward anything new, such as the younger or well-educated salespeople who enjoy respect from peers and can serve as opinion leaders, or those who have the potential to influence the behavior of the rest. In addition, a small-scale launch might allow for a detailed assessment of sales force perceptions regarding system functionalities or ease of use. The project committee should run a survey to gain insights into what salespeople regard as a barrier to using the system, what they fear most about it, and why they may hesitate to make full use of it. These insights can subsequently be used to take any necessary corrective actions before full system launch.

Activity 3: Launch the System in Full Scale

Launching the system in full scale represents one of the most critical activities in the entire implementation process, since this is the time at which the system must be accepted and used by all targeted users. During this "moment of truth," companies usually set up a date when the system goes "live" for all users throughout the organization. Companies may employ various methods for fostering excitement among users, such as organizing a series of events where salespeople share best practices with each other. Other companies have found it beneficial to develop promotional material that is subsequently administered to all users or used to announce the initiative through the company's newsletter. For instance, a large multinational organization operating in the pumping business has developed a DVD that uses cartoon characters to animate the system's capabilities and the daily life of a salesperson who uses the new system.

The difficulty of successfully launching the system may be so great that even if everything worked out in the right way during the preadoption stage or during the small-scale launch, there is no guarantee that the full-scale launch will succeed. The analogy of the difference between small- and full-scale launches resembles the situation where a swimmer prepares by practicing in a pool or lake and then goes to compete in the ocean. Likewise, success of the full-scale launch is contingent on many factors and parameters that may intervene in the process, especially in multibusiness or global companies. Managers need to make sure that intended benefits are visible to users and that any objections are identified and resolved. Also at this stage, users may feel uncertain as to how the system is embedded in, or affecting, their current work practices. Thus, the committee should facilitate users' understanding of the system functionalities by clearly communicating and demonstrating the value of the system.

The Postadoption Stage

The postadoption stage refers to the last stage in the implementation process. By now, users have accepted the system in their work and have started making use of it. While making users feel excited about the opportunity of sales technology was a major goal during the adoption stage, during the postadoption stage, management needs to work on getting users committed to using the technology. In other words, as discussed in chapter 2, successful implementation entails that users make use of the system in the most efficient and effective way.[14] Doing so necessitates that users find the best way to integrate and infuse the system into their current work practices. The following activities aim at assisting the project committee in achieving this objective.

Activity 1: Assisting Salespeople in Adjusting to the New Work Reality

It is during this stage where management must be ready to accept changes and make adjustments to the way salespeople work with the system in their daily activities. It is imperative to support users during their quest in finding the best ways of working with the system. This can be accomplished, for instance, by heavily investing in individualized training and user education workshops that demonstrate how the system can become an integral component of the sales job. Salespeople must understand how they can use the technology to increase their ability in adapting to specific customers' needs and to better serve customers, as these tasks can enhance their performance.[15]

Salespeople must also feel that the organization supports them even if their performance suffers from a sudden decline due to adjustments to the new work reality.[16] The project committee should allow for a period of experimentation with the system before performance gains are achieved. In particular, managers should move slowly by letting users understand the functionalities of the system and adjust to its existence. It takes time for technology to be fully integrated into an employee's routine behavior; sometimes, technology implementation can last a year or more, especially if the technology is targeted at multiple divisions or departments in a large and complex organization, or if it is perceived as being radically different than current systems and technologies. The goal is to excite, and thus encourage, users to adopt the system by getting them use the system on a frequent basis. One method that some firms have employed for making users feel more comfortable with using a system (e.g., a wireless SFA solution) is to give salespeople the opportunity to use the system for conducting personal or professional activities that may or may not be linked to their work per se. Examples include providing free access to subscribed databases or other content such as industry publications, newspapers, and professional magazines. Though such efforts should be implemented with extreme caution, they can nevertheless increase system familiarity and playfulness, which are important for accelerating adoption levels (see chapter 3). Nevertheless, the critical issue is to give users adequate time to familiarize themselves with the new reality and to adjust their working practices.

It is important to remember that some salespeople may be more inclined to adopt the technology early in the process and thus improve their performance through system usage. The role of the committee is to identify early successful cases and promote them throughout the entire sales organization. Publicizing cases of positive returns can spur adoption rates even among individuals who are not tech-savvy or are following a "wait-and-see" approach.

Activity 2: Close Monitoring of the Implementation Progress

To ensure that users will continue to use the system frequently enough so that it becomes integrated and infused into their current work practices, executives need to systematically monitor implementation progress. As discussed in chapter 2, it is the continued and committed use of the system that will lead to its infusion into a salesperson's job and, consequently, to improvements in individual performance. Even if initial user reactions toward the system are positive, or if users are using the system, this does not necessarily mean that users will keep up using it as time passes. Thus, management should ensure that users continue to use it after initial adoption.

Monitoring the progress of implementation can be accomplished through developing a dashboard of KPIs that allows for the assessment of each of the six key areas presented in detail in chapter 5: (a) system quality, (b) information quality, (c) service quality, (d) user satisfaction, (e) usage patterns, and (f) actualized benefits. The real challenge is to specify the nexus of metrics and KPIs that are most useful in a specific context. One particularly useful way of accomplishing this is to develop individualized reports concerning usage levels and achieved benefits that can be discussed during private face-to-face meetings between field supervisors and salespeople.

Summary

Successfully implementing a sales technology is a challenging task for all companies. Management has to carefully plan, communicate, and execute a great number of relevant activities. This chapter presented a comprehensive three-stage process of implementation that can be employed in order to get the most out of a sales technology investment. The process draws on the extant business and academic literature as well as on the author's own experiences. Each stage of the proposed implementation process comprises several activities that must be conducted in order to gain returns on investment. Collectively, the activities span the entire gamut of essential work that must be performed during system implementation: setting up a project committee, planning the process, deciding on whether to in-house or outsource the development of the system, working closely with the selected vendor, preparing system launch, launching the system in full-scale, assisting salespeople to adjust to the new reality, and closely monitoring progress throughout the entire lifetime of the project.

Notes

Preface

1. Speier and Venkatesh (2002).
2. Dickie (2006a).
3. Aberdeen Group (2009).
4. Damanpour (1991); Klein and Sorra (1996).

Chapter 1

1. Higgins, McIntyre, and Raine (1991).
2. McKee and Varadarajan (1995); Porter (1985).
3. Dewett and Jones (2001), p. 315.
4. Dewett and Jones (2001).
5. See, for instance, Anderson (1996) and Moncrief and Cravens (1999).
6. Band, Leaver, and Rogan (2008); Gartner (2009).
7. Hunter and Perreault (2007).
8. Parthasarathy and Sohi (1997), 196.
9. Rivers and Dart (1999), 59.
10. Erffmeyer and Johnson (2001), p. 168.
11. Morgan and Inks (2001), p. 463.
12. Speier and Venkatesh (2002), p. 99.
13. Engle and Barnes (2000), p. 219.
14. Honeycutt, Thelen, Thelen, and Hodge (2005), p. 313.
15. Srivastava, Shervani, and Fahey (1999), p. 169.
16. Reinartz, Krafft, and Hoyer (2004), p. 293.
17. Zablah, Bellenger, and Johnston (2004a), p. 475.
18. Payne and Frow (2005), p. 168.
19. Boulding, Staelin, Ehret, and Johnston (2005), p. 157.
20. Hunter and Perreault (2007), p. 17.
21. Manssen (1990); Morgan and Inks (2001); Moriarty and Swartz (1989); Rivers and Dart (1999).
22. Wedell and Hempeck (1987).
23. Hunter and Perreault (2007); Rapp, Agnihotri, and Forbes (2008).
24. Plouffe, Williams, and Leigh (2004).
25. Zablah et al. (2004a).
26. Buttle (2004).

27. Tanner, Ahearne, Leigh, Mason, and Moncrief (2005).

28. Tanner et al. (2005), p. 169.

29. Tanner et al. (2005), p. 169.

30. Tanner et al. (2005), p. 169–170.

31. See, for instance, Jayachandran, Sharma, Kaufman, and Raman (2005); Payne and Frow (2005); Reinartz et al. (2004); and Zablah, Bellenger, and Johnston (2004b).

32. Ahearne, Hughes, and Schillewaert (2007); Ahearne, Srinivasan, and Weinstein (2004).

33. Hunter and Perreault (2007); Jayachandran et al. (2005); Landry, Arnold, and Arndt (2005); Reinartz et al. (2004); Zablah et al. (2004b).

34. Hunter and Perreault (2007); Rapp, et al. (2008).

35. Rapp et al. (2008).

36. Morgan and Inks (2001); Krasnikov, Jayachandran, and Kumar (2009); Zablah et al. (2004b).

37. Srivastava et al. (1999).

38. Ahearne et al. (2004).

39. This term was coined by Hunter and Perreault (2007).

40. Hunter and Perreault (2007), p. 17.

41. Hunter and Perreault (2007).

42. Rapp et al. (2008).

43. Hunter and Perreault (2006), p. 96.

44. See, for instance, Collins (1988).

45. Collins (1984b).

46. Moncrief, Lamb, and Mackay (1991), p. 279.

47. Collins (1984b).

48. Caywood and Bauer (1986).

49. Busbin, Gross, and Dillon (1990); Comer (1981/1982); Hise and Reid (1994); Hughes (1983); Skiera and Albers (1998).

50. Collins, Carey, and Mauritson (1987); Heschel (1977); Strout (1999).

51. Collins (1985b).

52. See the CALLPLAN program by Lodish (1971).

53. Stevenson, Plath, and Bush (1990).

54. Steinberg and Plank (1987).

55. See, for instance, Collins (1984a) and Hennessey (1988).

56. Collins and Mauritson (1987).

57. Coppett and Voorhees (1985), p. 214.

58. See, for instance, Marshall and Vredenburg (1988) and Moncrief, Shipp, Lamb, and Cravens (1989).

59. See, for instance, Caywood and Bauer (1986).

60. Hill and Swenson (1994), p. 80.

61. Stevenson et al. (1990), p. 243.

62. Dishman and Aytes (1996), p. 66.

63. Collins (1984b), p. 75.

64. Collins (1984b), p. 75.

65. See, for instance, Collins (1985a).

66. Coppett and Voorhees (1985), p. 214.

67. Hill and Swenson (1994); Iacovou, Benbasat, and Dexter (1995).

68. See, for instance, Long, Tellefsen, and Lichtenthal (2007).

69. See, for instance, Samli, Wills, and Herbig (1997).

70. Swenson and Parrella (1992).

71. See, for instance, Collins (1986).

72. Martin and Collins (1991).

73. Honeycutt, McCarty, and Howe (1993).

74. Dishman and Aytes (1996).

75. See Hunter and Perreault (2007).

76. See, for instance, Engle and Barnes (2000); Hunter and Perreault (2007); Marshall, Moncrief, and Lassk (1999); and Widmier, Jackson, and McCabe (2002).

77. Hill and Swenson (1994).

78. Raghunathan and Yeh (2001), p. 406.

79. See, for instance, Anderson (1996); Manssen (1990); and Moriarty and Swartz (1989).

80. Strout (1999).

81. Brady, Saren, and Tzokas (1999).

82. Hunter and Perreault (2007).

83. Ahearne and Rapp (in press).

84. Speier and Venkatesh (2002).

85. Gartner (2009).

86. The vendor list draws primarily from the work of Beal (2007) and Edwards (2007) and represents an effort to illustrate the variety of offerings in the market. Importantly, however, the list is neither inclusive nor does it aim at favoring one or more vendors.

Chapter 2

1. See, for instance, Speier and Venkatesh (2002).

2. Klein, Conn, and Sorra (2001), p. 811.

3. Rogers (1995), p. 21.

4. Klein and Sorra (1996), p. 1057.

5. Cooper and Zmud (1990), p. 124.

6. Frambach and Schillewaert (2002), p. 164.

7. See, inter alia, Cooper and Zmud (1990); Klein and Sorra (1996); Klein et al. (2001); Lewin (1952); Shih and Venkatesh (2004); and Sundaram, Schwarz, Jones, and Chin (2007).

8. Cooper and Zmud (1990).

9. Shih and Venkatesh (2004).

10. Lewin (1952).

11. See, for instance, Ahearne, Lam, Mathieu, and Bolander (in press) and Cooper and Zmud (1990).

12. Klein and Sorra (1996).

13. Klein and Sorra (1996), p. 1057.

14. Sundaram et al. (2007).

15. See, inter alia, Damanpour (1991) and Rogers (1983).

16. Klein and Sorra (1996).

17. See also Jasperson, Carter, and Zmud (2005).

18. Frambach and Schillewaert (2002); Jasperson et al. (2005); Parthasarathy and Sohi (1997).

19. Parthasarathy and Sohi (1997).

20. Parthasarathy and Sohi (1997), p. 197.

21. Klein and Sorra (1996).

22. Cooper and Zmud (1990); Sundaram et al. (2007); Schillewaert, Ahearne, Frambach, and Moenaert (2005).

23. Klein and Sorra (1996), p. 1058.

24. Zmud and Apple (1992).

25. Sundaram et al. (2007).

26. Ahearne, Srinivasan, and Weinstein (2004).

27. Senecal, Pullins, and Buehrer (2007).

28. Selection of models is primarily guided by the work of Venkatesh, Morris, Davis, and Davis (2003); their work offers an exhaustive review and synthesis of prior IT-acceptance research.

29. See Ajzen and Fishbein (1980) and Fishbein and Ajzen (1975).

30. See, for instance, Davis, Bagozzi, and Warshaw (1989) and Sundaram et al. (2007).

31. Fishbein and Ajzen (1975), p. 288.

32. Fishbein and Ajzen (1975), p. 216.

33. Fishbein and Ajzen (1975), p. 302.

34. Mediation refers to the phenomenon where the influence of one variable on another is not direct but rather through some other variable or process.

35. Bagozzi, Baumgartner, and Yi (1992), p. 505.

36. Davis et al. (1989).

37. Moderation involves the phenomenon where the strength or direction of the relationship between two variables is affected by a third variable or condition.

38. Karahanna, Straub, and Shervany (1999).

39. Davis (1986).

40. Davis (1989), p. 320.

41. Davis (1989), p. 320.

42. Davis et al. (1989), p. 986.

43. Davis et al. (1989).

44. Venkatesh and Morris (2000).

45. See, for instance, Davis et al. (1989) and Pavlou (2002).

46. King and He (2006); Schepers and Wetzels (2007).

47. See, for instance, Avlonitis and Panagopoulos (2005); Jones, Sundaram, and Chin (2002); Robinson, Marshall, and Stamps (2005a); Schillewaert et al. (2005); Sun and Zhang (2006); and Sundaram et al. (2007).

48. See, for instance, Benbasat and Barki (2007).

49. Venkatesh and Davis (2000).

50. Schepers and Wetzels (2007).

51. Venkatesh and Davis (2000), p. 188.

52. Moore and Benbasat (1991), p. 203.

53. Davis et al. (1992).

54. Davis et al. (1992), p. 1113.

55. See, for instance, Calder and Staw (1975).

56. Davis et al. (1992), p. 1112.

57. Davis et al. (1992), p. 1112.

58. Davis et al. (1992).

59. Ajzen (1985, 1989).

60. See, for example, the meta-analytic review by Armitage and Conner (2001).

61. Mathieson (1991).

62. Taylor and Todd (1995b), p. 149.

63. Mathieson (1991).

64. Mathieson (1991).

65. Mathieson (1991), p. 176.

66. Mathieson (1991), p. 176.

67. Mathieson (1991), p. 176.

68. Mathieson (1991), p. 176.

69. Mathieson (1991), p. 176.

70. See, for instance, Morris and Venkatesh (2000) and Venkatesh, Morris, and Ackerman (2000).

71. Taylor and Todd (1995a).

72. Taylor and Todd (1995a).

73. Thompson, Higgins, and Howell (1991).

74. Triandis (1980).

75. Venkatesh et al. (2003).

76. Triandis (1980).

77. Thompson et al. (1991), p. 129.

78. Thompson et al. (1991), p. 129.

79. Rogers and Shoemaker (1971), p. 154.

80. Triandis (1980), p. 211.

81. Triandis (1980), p. 210.

82. Thompson et al. (1991), p. 126.

83. Triandis (1980), p. 205.

84. Thompson et al. (1991).

85. Thompson et al. (1994).

86. Rogers (1983).

87. Moore and Benbasat (1991).

88. Moore and Benbasat (1991), p. 195–203.

89. Karahanna et al. (1999).

90. See Bandura (1986) for a description of the social cognitive theory.

91. Compeau and Higgins (1995b).

92. Compeau and Higgins (1995b), p. 192.

93. Compeau and Higgins (1995b), p. 195.

94. Compeau and Higgins (1995b).

95. Compeau and Higgins (1995a).

96. Venkatesh et al. (2003).

97. Venkatesh et al. (2003), p. 447.

98. Venkatesh et al. (2003), p. 450.

99. Venkatesh et al. (2003), p. 451.

100. Venkatesh et al. (2003), p. 453.

101. Venkatesh et al. (2003).

102. See, for instance, the meta-analysis by King and He (2006).

103. See, inter alia, Alavi and Joachimsthaler (1992); Avlonitis and Panagopoulos (2005); Frambach and Schillewaert (2002); Jones et al. (2002); Schillewaert, Ahearne, Frambach, and Moenaert (2000); Schillewaert et al. (2005); Speier and Venkatesh (2002); and Sun and Zhang (2006).

Chapter 3

1. See Moore and Benbasat (1991) and Rogers (1983).

2. Rothman (1974), p. 441.

3. Rogers and Shoemaker (1971), p. 155.

4. Parthasarathy and Sohi (1997).

5. Gohmann, Barker, Faulds, and Guan (2005).

6. Moore and Benbasat (1991); Tornatzky and Klein (1982).

7. Rothman (1974), p. 441.

8. Jones, Sundaram, and Chin (2002); Kim and Srivastava (1998); Speier and Venkatesh (2002).

9. Tornatzky and Klein (1982), p. 33.

10. Kim and Srivastava (1998); Parthasarathy and Sohi (1997); Speier and Venkatesh (2002).

11. Rogers and Shoemaker (1971), p. 154.

12. Gohmann, Barker, Faulds, and Guan (2005).

13. Kim and Srivastava (1998); Moore and Benbasat (1991).

14. Rogers and Shoemaker (1971), p. 155.

15. Avlonitis and Panagopoulos (2005); Homburg, Wieseke, and Kuehnl (in press); Jones et al. (2002); Robinson, Marshall, and Stamps (2005a); Schillewaert, Ahearne, Frambach, and Moenaert (2005).

16. Davis (1989), p. 320.

17. Avlonitis and Panagopoulos (2005); Homburg et al. (in press); Jones et al. (2002); Rangarajan, Jones, and Chin (2005); Robinson et al. (2005a); Schillewaert et al. (2005).

18. Davis (1989), p. 320.

19. Speier and Venkatesh (2002); Zablah, Bellenger, and Johnston (2004b).

20. Agarwal and Prasad (1997), p. 564.

21. Speier and Venkatesh (2002).

22. Speier and Venkatesh (2002), p. 102.

23. Speier and Venkatesh (2002).

24. Rogers and Shoemaker (1971), p. 138.

25. Moore and Benbasat (1991).

26. Fliegel, Kivlin, and Sekhon (1967), p. 445.

27. Speier and Venkatesh (2002).

28. Rogers and Shoemaker (1971), p. 155.

29. See, for instance, Avlonitis and Panagopoulos (2005); Jones et al. (2002); Mallin and DelVecchio (2008); Rangarajan et al. (2005); Robinson et al. (2005a); Schillewaert et al. (2005).

30. Honeycutt et al. (2005).

31. See, for instance, Barker, Gohmann, Guan, and Faulds (2009); Gohmann, Guan, Barker, and Faulds (2005).

32. Jones et al. (2002).

33. Agarwal and Prasad (1997).

34. Speier and Venkatesh (2002); Zablah et al. (2004b).

35. Speier and Venkatesh (2002).

36. Speier and Venkatesh (2002).

37. Agarwal and Prasad (1997); Tornatzky and Klein (1982).

38. Alavi and Joachimsthaler (1992).

39. See, for instance, Alavi and Joachimsthaler (1992); Agarwal and Prasad (1999); Keillor, Bashaw, and Pettijohn (1997); Parthasarathy and Sohi (1997); Speier and Venkatesh (2002); and Zablah et al. (2004b).

150 NOTES

40. See, for instance, Barker et al. (2009); Buehrer, Senecal, and Pullins (2005); Hunter and Perreault (2006); Lapierre and Denier (2005); Robinson, Marshall, and Stamps (2005b); and Senecal et al. (2007).

41. Keillor et al. (1997).

42. Speier and Venkatesh (2002); Zablah et al. (2004b).

43. Barker et al. (2009); Hunter and Perreault (2006); Parthasarathy and Sohi (1997); Speier and Venkatesh (2002); Zablah et al. (2004b).

44. Parthasarathy and Sohi (1997); Zablah et al. (2004b).

45. Alavi and Joachimsthaler (1992); Avlonitis and Panagopoulos (2005); Frambach and Schillewaert (2002); Parthasarathy and Sohi (1997); Senecal et al. (2007); Zablah et al. (2004b).

46. Speier and Venkatesh (2002); Zablah et al. (2004b).

47. Speier and Venkatesh (2002).

48. Webster and Martocchio (1992), p. 204.

49. Avlonitis and Panagopoulos (2005); Kwahk and Lee (2008); Mathieu, Ahearne, and Taylor (2007); Morgan and Inks (2001); Schillewaert et al. (2005); Speier and Venkatesh (2002).

50. Compeau and Higgins (1995b), p. 192.

51. Barker et al. (2009); Bush, Bush, Orr, and Rocco (2007); Gohmann, Guan, Barker, and Faulds (2005); Honeycutt et al. (2005); Morgan and Inks (2001); Rivers and Dart (1999); Sviokla (1996).

52. Geiger and Turley (2006); Honeycutt et al. (2005); Johnson and Bharadwaj (2005); Tanner and Shipp (2005).

53. Geiger and Turley (2006); Honeycutt et al. (2005); Morgan and Inks (2001); Sviokla (1996).

54. Cho and Chang (2008).

55. Churchill, Ford, and Walker (1974), p. 255.

56. Jelinek, Ahearne, Mathieu, and Schillewaert (2006); Raman, Wittmann, and Rauseo (2006); Schillewaert et al. (2005).

57. Dweck and Leggett (1988), p. 256.

58. Jelinek et al. (2006).

59. Dweck and Leggett (1988), p. 256.

60. Avlonitis and Panagopoulos (2005); Cho and Chang (2008); Frambach and Schillewaert (2002); Jones et al. (2002); Robinson et al. (2005b); Senecal et al. (2007); Schillewaert et al. (2005).

61. Agarwal and Prasad (1998), p. 206.

62. Cho and Chang (2008); Kim and Srivastava (1998); Parthasarathy and Sohi (1997); Petouhoff (2006).

63. Kwahk and Lee (2008), p. 475.

64. Honeycutt et al. (2005); Rangarajan et al. (2005), p. 349; Speier and Venkatesh (2002).

65. Honeycutt et al. (2005); Rangarajan et al. (2005); Speier and Venkatesh (2002).

66. Webster and Martocchio (1992).

67. Speier and Venkatesh (2002).

68. Campbell (1998).

69. Morgan and Inks (2001).

70. Compeau and Higgins (1995b).

71. Avlonitis and Panagopoulos (2005); Mathieu et al. (2007); Schillewaert et al. (2000, 2005).

72. Bandura (1977).

73. Mathieu et al. (2007).

74. Ostrow (2008).

75. Dubinsky, Howell, Ingram, and Bellenger (1986).

76. Mulki, Locander, Marshall, Harris, and Hensel (2008).

77. Barker et al. (2009); Bush et al. (2007); Gohmann, Guan, Barker, and Faulds (2005); Morgan and Inks (2001).

78. See, for instance, Morgan and Inks (2001) and Rivers and Dart (1999).

79. Honeycutt et al. (2005).

80. See, for instance, Geiger and Turley (2006).

81. Barker et al. (2009); Honeycutt et al. (2005).

82. Honeycutt et al. (2005); Johnson and Bharadwaj (2005).

83. Honeycutt et al. (2005).

84. Barker et al. (2009); Honeycutt et al. (2005).

85. Palmatier, Scheer, and Steenkamp (2007).

86. Honeycutt et al. (2005).

87. See, for instance, Honeycutt et al. (2005) and Sviokla (1996).

88. Geiger and Turley (2006).

89. Morgan and Inks (2001).

90. Cho and Chang (2008).

91. Raman et al. (2006); Sujan, Weitz, and Kumar (1994).

92. Jelinek et al. (2006).

93. Rogers (1983).

94. Agarwal and Prasad (1998), p. 206.

95. Cho and Chang (2008).

96. Robinson et al. (2005b).

97. Schillewaert et al. (2005).

98. Frambach and Schillewaert (2002).

99. Agarwal and Prasad (1998); Avlonitis and Panagopoulos (2005); Jones et al. (2002).

100. Senecal et al. (2007).

101. Petouhoff (2006).

102. See, for instance, Kim and Srivastava (1998).

103. Kwahk and Lee (2008).

104. Kwahk and Lee (2008), p. 475.

105. Kwahk and Lee (2008), p. 475.

106. Honeycutt et al. (2005); Rangarajan et al. (2005).

107. Singh (1998).

108. Rangarajan et al. (2005).

109. Rangarajan et al. (2005).

110. Speier and Venkatesh (2002).

111. Klein and Sorra (1996), p. 1060.

112. Pullig, Maxham, and Hair (2002).

113. Goldenberg (2006); Morgan and Inks (2001); Rasmusson (1999); Speier and Venkatesh (2002).

114. Barker et al. (2009).

115. Dickie (2006a); Jelinek et al. (2006); Robinson et al. (2005b); Pullig et al. (2002); Schillewaert et al. (2005).

116. Parthasarathy and Sohi (1997).

117. See, for instance, Buehrer et al. (2005); Bush, Moore, and Rocco (2005); Hunter and Perreault (2006, 2007); Pullig et al. (2002); and Schillewaert et al. (2005).

118. Erffmeyer and Johnson (2001).

119. Morgan and Inks (2001).

120. Pullig et al. (2002).

121. Jelinek et al. (2006).

122. Agarwal, Harding, and Schumacher (2004); Frambach and Schillewaert (2002); Radcliffe (2001).

123. Bhattacherjee (1998).

124. Lapierre and Denier (2005).

125. Ahearne et al. (2004).

126. Klein and Sorra (1996); Pullig et al. (2002).

127. Klein and Sorra (1996), p. 1060.

128. Barker et al. (2009); Kim and Srivastava (1998); Morgan and Inks (2001); Pae, Kim, Han, and Yip (2002); Rasmusson (1999); Rivers and Dart (1999); Speier and Venkatesh (2002).

129. Jarvenpaa and Ives (1991), p. 206.

130. Buehrer et al. (2005); Dickie (2006a); Frambach and Schillewaert (2002); Homburg et al. (in press); Jelinek et al. (2006); Parthasarathy and Sohi (1997); Rasmusson (1999); Pullig et al. (2002); Robinson et al. (2005b); Schillewaert et al. (2005).

131. Alavi and Joachimsthaler (1992); Avlonitis and Panagopoulos (2005); Buehrer et al. (2005); Bush et al. (2005); Dickie (2006a); Errmeyer and Johnson (2001); Frambach and Schillewaert (2002); Gohmann, Guan, Barker, and Faulds (2005); Homburg et al. (in press); Hunter and Perreault (2006, 2007); Jelinek

et al. (2006); Morgan and Inks (2001); Pullig et al. (2002); Rasmusson (1999); Schillewaert et al. (2005); Zablah et al (2004b).

132. Agarwal et al. (2004); Chang, Park, and Chaiy (in press); Frambach and Schillewaert (2002); Bhattacherjee (1998); Radcliffe (2001).

133. Honeycutt et al. (2005); Rasmusson (1999); Rigby, Reichheld, and Schefter (2002).

134. Alavi and Joachimsthaler (1992); Avlonitis and Panagopoulos (2005); Morgan and Inks (2001); Rasmusson (1999); Speier and Venkatesh (2002); Zablah et al. (2004b).

135. Hartwick and Barki (1994), p. 441.

136. Avlonitis and Panagopoulos (2005); Damanpour (1991); Honeycutt et al. (2005); Morgan and Inks (2001); Zablah et al. (2004b).

137. Lapierre and Denier (2005); Morgan and Inks (2001); Rigby et al. (2002); Zablah et al. (2004b).

138. Raman et al. (2006).

139. Raman et al. (2006), p. 47.

140. Damanpour (1991); Kim and Srivastava (1998); Papastathopoulou, Avlonitis, and Panagopoulos (2007); Parthasarathy and Sohi (1997); Zmud (1982).

141. Rogers (1983), p. 359.

142. Damanpour (1991); Kim and Srivastava (1998); Papastathopoulou et al. (2007); Zmud (1982).

143. Rogers (1983), p. 360.

144. Erffmeyer and Johnson (2001); Kim and Srivastava (1998).

145. Chang et al. (in press); Jayachandran et al. (2005); Pullig et al. (2002); Raman et al. (2006); Richard, Thirkell, and Huff (2007); Zablah et al. (2004b).

146. Deshpandé, Farley, and Webster (1993), p. 27.

147. Frambach and Schillewaert (2002); Robinson et al. (2005b).

148. Honeycutt et al. (2005).

149. See, for instance, Rasmusson (1999).

150. Rigby et al. (2002).

151. Avlonitis and Panagopoulos (2005).

152. Rasmusson (1999).

153. Honeycutt et al. (2005).

154. Morgan and Inks (2001).

155. Alavi and Joachimsthaler (1992).

156. See, for instance, Lapierre and Denier (2005); Rigby et al. (2002); and Zablah et al. (2004b).

157. Honeycutt et al. (2005).

158. Damanpour (1991); Honeycutt et al. (2005).

159. Jimmieson, Peach, and White (2008).

160. Avlonitis and Panagopoulos (2005); Damanpour (1991); Morgan and Inks (2001).

161. Zablah et al. (2004b).

162. Rigby et al. (2002).

163. Raman et al. (2006).

164. See, inter alia, Damanpour (1991); Kim and Srivastava (1998); Papastathopoulou et al. (2007); Parthasarathy and Sohi (1997); and Zmud (1982).

165. Damanpour (1991); Kim and Srivastava (1998); Papastathopoulou et al. (2007); Zmud (1982).

166. Kim and Srivastava (1998).

167. See, for instance, Zaltman, Duncan, and Holbek (1973).

168. Walton and Dutton (1969), p. 73.

169. Kim and Srivastava (1998).

170. Jaworski and Kohli (1993), pp. 55–56.

171. Erffmeyer and Johnson (2001); Kim and Srivastava (1998).

172. Erffmeyer and Johnson (2001).

173. Chang et al. (in press); Pullig et al. (2002); Raman et al. (2006); Richard et al. (2007); Zablah et al. (2004b).

174. See, for instance, Frambach and Schillewaert (2002); Lapierre and Denier (2005); Robinson et al. 2005b; and Senecal et al. (2007).

175. Kim and Srivastava (1998); Pae et al. (2002); Parthasarathy and Sohi (1997); Robertson and Gatignon (1986).

176. Gatignon and Roberston (1989); Kim and Srivastava (1998); Parthasarathy and Sohi (1997); Roberston and Gatignon (1986).

177. Frambach and Schillewaert (2002); Gatignon and Robertson (1989); Robertson and Gatignon (1986).

178. Frambach and Schillewaert (2002).

179. Avlonitis and Panagopoulos (2005); Hunter and Perreault (2006, 2007); Homburg et al. (in press); Jelinek et al. (2006); Jones et al. (2002); Pullig et al. (2002); Schillewaert et al. (2005).

180. Hunter and Perreault (2006, 2007).

181. Parthasarathy and Sohi (1997).

182. Homburg et al. (in press); Mathieu et al. (2007).

183. Kim and Srivastava (1998); Pae et al. (2002); Parthasarathy and Sohi (1997); Robertson and Gatignon (1986).

184. Jaworski and Kohli (1993), p. 57.

185. Kim and Srivastava (1998); Pae et al. (2002).

186. Jaworski and Kohli (1993), p. 57.

187. Frambach and Schillewaert (2002); Gatignon and Robertson (1989); Kim and Srivastava (1998); Robertson and Gatignon (1986); Seiders et al. (2005).

188. Seiders, Voss, Grewal, and Godfrey (2005), p. 31.

189. Frambach and Schillewaert (2002); Hunter and Perreault (2006, 2007); Jelinek et al. (2006); Jones et al. (2002); Schillewaert et al. (2005).

190. Avlonitis and Panagopoulos (2005); Frambach and Schillewaert (2002); Jelinek et al. (2006); Jones et al. (2002); Schillewaert et al. (2005).

191. Avlonitis and Panagopoulos (2005); Cho and Chang (2008); Frambach and Schillewaert (2002); Homburg et al. (in press); Jelinek et al. (2006); Jones et al. (2002); Parthasarathy and Sohi (1997); Schillewaert et al. (2005).

192. Avlonitis and Panagopoulos (2005); Frambach and Schillewaert (2002); Homburg et al. (in press); Mathieu et al. (2007); Pullig et al. (2002); Schillewaert et al. (2005).

193. Raman et al. (2006).

194. Goodhue and Thompson (1995), p. 216.

195. Raman et al. (2006).

196. Raman et al. (2006).

197. See, for instance, Steenkamp, Hofstede, and Wedel (1999); Veiga, Floyd, and Dechant (2001).

198. Hofstede (1980).

199. Veiga et al. (2001).

200. Veiga et al. (2001).

201. Strite (2006).

202. Schepers and Wetzels (2007), p. 100.

203. Strite (2006).

204. For more details on privacy issues across countries, visit http://www.privireal.org/content/dp/countries.php

Chapter 4

1. See, for instance, Byrd and Marshall (1997) and Cron and Sobol (1983).

2. See, for instance, Good and Stone (2000) and Moriarty and Swartz (1989).

3. See, for instance, Brynjolfsson (1993) and Hitt and Brynjolfsson (1996).

4. Brynjolfsson and Yang (1996).

5. See also Johannessen, Olaisen, and Olsen (1999).

6. Byrd and Marshall (1997); Hitt and Brynjolfsson (1996).

7. See the meta-analysis by Kohli and Devaraj (2003).

8. Li and Ye (1999).

9. Lucas (1975).

10. Cron and Sobol (1983).

11. Kivijärvi and Saarinen (1995).

12. Powell and Dent-Micallef (1997).

13. Kivijärvi and Saarinen (1995).

14. See also Good and Stone (2000).

15. See, for instance, Brynjolfsson and Hitt (1998) and Gunasekaran, Love, Rahimi, and Miele (2001).

16. Prattipati and Mensah (1997); Stratopoulos and Dehning (2000); Teo and Wong (1998).

17. Lee (2001).

18. Bharadwaj, Bharadwaj, and Konsynski (1999).

19. Andersen (2001); Andersen and Segars (2001); Dewett and Jones (2001); Kivijärvi and Saarinen (1995); Lee (2001); Li and Ye (1999); Teo and Wong (1998).

20. Dehning and Richardson (2002).

21. Brynjolfsson and Yang (1996).

22. Igbaria and Tan (1997); Klein and Sorra (1996).

23. Davis, Bagozzi, and Warshaw (1989); DeLone and McLean (1992); Johannessen et al. (1999); Straub, Limayem, and Karahanna-Evaristo (1995); Thompson, Higgins, and Howell (1991).

24. Goodhue, Klein, and March (2000).

25. Goodhue and Thompson (1995).

26. Stratopoulos and Dehning (2000).

27. DeLone and McLean (1992).

28. Petter and McLean (2009), p. 161.

29. DeLone and McLean (1992), p. 62.

30. DeLone and McLean (2003).

31. Klein and Sorra (1996).

32. Mahmood, Burn, Gemoets, and Jacquez (2000); Petter and McLean (2009).

33. DeLone and McLean (2003).

34. Petter and McLean (2009), p. 161.

35. Petter and McLean (2009), p. 161.

36. Petter and McLean (2009), p. 161.

37. See DeLone and McLean (2003) for a review of studies that have employed the D&MM.

38. Etezadi-Amoli and Farhoomad (1996).

39. Igbaria and Tan (1997).

40. Gelderman (1998).

41. Avlonitis and Panagopoulos (2005).

42. Petter and McLean (2009).

43. See, for instance, Marinova, Ye, and Singh (2008); Ostroff and Schmitt (1993); and Quinn and Rohrbaugh (1981).

44. Collins (1987); Golany and Tamir (1995).

45. Golany and Tamir (1995), p. 1172.

46. See, for instance, Collins (1987).

47. Drucker (1974), p. 572.

48. Sheth and Sisodia (2002), p. 351.

49. See, inter alia, Andersen (2001); Ahearne, Jelinek, and Rapp (2005); Cravens, Grant, Ingram, LaForge, and Young (1992); Cravens, Ingram, LaForge, and Young (1992); Dickie (2006b); Erffmeyer and Johnson (2001); Hise and Reid (1994); Hughes (1983); Hunter and Perreault (2007); Moncrief et al. (1991); Moriarty and Swartz (1989); Rivers and Dart (1999); and Sundaram et al. (2007).

50. *CRM Magazine* (2007).

51. Krigsman (2009); Zablah et al. (2004b).

52. Brynjolfsson and Hitt (2003).

53. Moriarty and Swartz (1989); Wedell and Hempeck (1987).

54. See, for instance, Hunter and Perreault (2007); Moutot and Bascoul (2008).

55. Ahearne et al. (2004).

56. Sundaram et al. (2007).

57. Ahearne, Jones, Rapp, and Mathieu (2008); Ahearne et al. (2007); Hunter and Perreault (2006, 2007); Park, Kim, Dubinsky, and Lee (in press); Rapp et al. (2008); Robinson et al. (2005a).

58. Ahearne et al. (2005); Ko and Dennis (2004); Mathieu et al. (2007).

59. See, for instance, Buehrer et al. (2005); Erffmeyer and Johnson (2001); Lapierre and Denier (2005); and Moncrief et al. (1991).

60. Gupta and Zeithaml (2006); Rust, Ambler, Carpenter, Kumar, and Srivastava (2004).

Chapter 5

1. Bohling et al. (2006).

2. See, for instance, Ahearne, Jones, Rapp, and Mathieu (2008); Hunter and Perreault (2007); and Sundaram, Schwarz, Jones, and Chni (2007).

3. See, for instance, Honeycutt, Thelen, Thelen, and Hodge (2005) and Tanner, Ahearne, Leigh, Mason, and Moncrief (2005).

4. *CRM Magazine* (2007); Erffmeyer and Johnson (2001).

5. Klein and Sorra (1996).

6. Klein and Sorra (1996), p. 1058.

7. Klein and Sorra (1996); Sundaram et al. (2007).

8. See, for instance, DeLone and McLean (1992, 2003); Dickie (2006b); and Zablah, Bellenger, and Johnson (2004a).

9. DeLone and McLean (2003).

10. Pauwels et al. (2009).

11. DeLone and McLean (1992), p. 80.

12. Ahearne, Srinivasan, and Weinstein (2004).

13. Rigby, Reichheld, and Schefter (2002).

14. Ahearne, Jelinek, and Rapp (2005); Erffmeyer and Johnson (2001).

15. Chang, Park, and Chaiy (in press).

16. Krasnikov, Jayachandran, and Kumar (2009).

17. Hendricks, Singhal, and Stratman (2007).

18. Srivastava, Shervani, and Fahey (1999).

19. Rust, Ambler, Carpenter, Kumar, and Srivastava (2004), p. 79.

20. Kirpalani and Shapiro (1973).

21. Engle and Barnes (2000).

22. Buttle, Ang, and Iriana (2006).

23. Ang and Buttle (2002); Dugan (1998); Hendricks, Singhal, and Stratman (2007).

Chapter 6

1. Bush, Moore, and Rocco (2005).

2. McKay (2009).

3. McKay (2009).

4. McKay (2009).

5. Bush, Bush, Orr, and Rocco (2007).

6. Parthasarathy and Sohi (1997).

7. Compton (2003).

8. Compton (2003).

9. McKay (2009).

10. Compton (2003).

11. Compton (2003).

12. Dickie (2006a).

13. McKay (2009).

14. See, for instance, Cooper and Zmud (1990); Jones, Sundaram, and Chin (2002); and Sundaram, Schwarz, Jones, and Chin (2007).

15. Ahearne, Jones, Rapp, and Mathieu (2008).

16. Ahearne, Lam, Mathieu, and Bolander (in press).

References

Aberdeen Group. (2009). *The 2009 SFA report: Best-in-class strategies for increasing returns on SFA investments.* Retrieved January 1C, 2010, from http://www.aberdeen.com/launch/report/research_previews/6139-RP-sales-force-automation.asp

Agarwal, A., Harding, D. P., & Schumacher, J. R. (2004). Organizing for CRM. *McKinsey Quarterly, 3,* 80–91.

Agarwal, R., & Prasad, J. (1997). The role of innovation characteristics and perceived voluntariness in the acceptance of information technologies. *Decision Sciences, 28*(3), 557–580.

Agarwal, R., & Prasad, J. (1998). A conceptual and operational definition of personal innovativeness in the domain of information technology. *Information Systems Research, 9*(2), 204–215.

Agarwal, R., & Prasad, J. (1999). Are individual differences germane to the acceptance of new information technologies? *Decision Sciences, 30*(2), 361–391.

Ahearne, M., & Rapp, A. (in press). Business to consumer selling technologies: For better or worse—"til death do we part." *Journal of Personal Selling & Sales Management.*

Ahearne, M., Hughes, D. E., & Schillewaert, N. (2007) Why sales representatives should welcome information technology: Measuring the impact of CRM-based IT on sales effectiveness. *International Journal of Research in Marketing, 24*(4), 336–349.

Ahearne, M., Jelinek, R., & Rapp, A. (2005). Moving beycnd the direct effect of SFA adoption on salesperson performance: Training and support as key moderating factors. *Industrial Marketing Management, 34*(4), 379–388.

Ahearne, M., Jones, E., Rapp, A., & Mathieu, J. (2008). High touch through high tech: The impact of salesperson technology usage on sales performance via mediating mechanisms. *Management Science, 54*(4), 671–685.

Ahearne, M., Lam, S. K., Mathieu, J. E., & Bolander, W. (in press). Why are some salespeople better at adapting to organizational change? *Journal of Marketing.*

Ahearne, M., Srinivasan, N., & Weinstein, L. (2004). Effect of technology on sales performance: Progressing from technology acceptance to technology usage and consequence. *Journal of Personal Selling & Sales Management, 24*(4), 297–310.

Ajzen, I. (1985). From intentions to actions: A theory of planned behavior. In J. Kuhl & J. Beekmann (Eds.), *Action control: From cognition to behavior* (pp. 11–39). New York, NY: Springer Verlag.

Ajzen, I. (1989). Attitude structure and behavior. In A. R. Pratkanis., S. J. Breckler, & A. G. Greenwald (Eds.), *Attitude structure and function* (pp. 241–274). Hillsdale, NJ: Lawrence Erlbaum Associates.

Ajzen, I., & Fishbein, M. (1980). *Understanding attitudes and predicting social behavior*. Englewood Cliffs, NJ: Prentice-Hall.

Alavi, M., & Joachimsthaler, E. A. (1992). Revisiting DSS implementation research: A meta-analysis of the literature and suggestions for researchers. *MIS Quarterly, 16*(1), 95–116.

Andersen, T. J. (2001). Information technology, strategic decision making approaches and organizational performance in different industrial settings. *Journal of Strategic Information Systems, 10*(2), 101–119.

Andersen, T. J., & Segars, A. H. (2001). The impact of IT on decision structure and firm performance: Evidence from the textile and apparel industry. *Information and Management, 39*(2), 85–100.

Anderson, R. E. (1996). Personal selling and sales management in the new millennium. *Journal of Personal Selling and Sales Management, 16*(4), 17–32.

Ang, L., & Buttle, F. (2002). *ROI on CRM, a customer-journey approach*. Conference Proceedings of IMP Conference, Perth, Australia.

Armitage, C. J., & Conner, M. (2001). Efficacy of the theory of planned behavior: A meta-analytic review. *British Journal of Social Psychology, 40*(4), 471–499.

Avlonitis, G. J., & Panagopoulos, N. G. (2005). Antecedents and consequences of CRM technology acceptance in the sales force. *Industrial Marketing Management, 34*(4), 355–368.

Bagozzi, R. P., Baumgartner, H., & Yi, Y. (1992). State versus action orientation and the theory of reasoned action: An application to coupon usage. *Journal of Consumer Research, 18*(4), 505–518.

Band, W., Leaver, S., & Rogan, M. A. (2008). *CRM best practices adoption*. Retrieved December 16, 2009, from http://www.forrester.com/rb/Research/crm_best_practices_adoption/q/id/44179/t/2

Bandura, A. (1986). *Social foundations of thought and action: A social cognition theory*. Englewood Cliffs, NJ: Prentice-Hall.

Bandura, A. (1977). Self-efficacy: Toward a unifying theory of behavioral change. *Psychological Review, 84*(2), 191–215.

Barker, R. M., Gohmann, S. F., Guan, J., & Faulds, D. J. (2009). Why is my sales force automation system failing? *Business Horizons, 52*(3), 233–241.

Beal, B. (2007). *Top 15 CRM vendors, emerging trends revealed.* Retrieved December 16, 2009, from http://searchcrm.techtarget.com/news/1249200/Top-15-CRM-vendors-emerging-trends-revealed

Benbasat, I., & Barki, H. (2007). Quo vadis, TAM? *Journal of the Association for Information Systems, 8*(4), 211–218.

Bharadwaj, A., Bharadwaj, S., & Konsynski, B. (1999). Information technology effects on firm performance as measured by Tobin's *q*. *Management Science, 45*(7), 1008–1024.

Bhattacherjee, A. (1998). Managerial influences on intra-organizational information technology use: A principal-agent model. *Decision Sciences, 29*(1), 139–162.

Bohling, T., Bowman, D., LaValle, S., Mittal, V., Narayandas, D., Ramani, G., & Varadarajan, R. (2006). CRM implementation: Effectiveness issues and insights. *Journal of Service Research, 9*(2), 184–194.

Boulding, W., Staelin, R., Ehret, M., & Johnston, W. J. (2005). A customer relationship management roadmap: What is known, potential pitfalls, and where to go. *Journal of Marketing, 69*(4), 155–166.

Brady, M., Saren, M., & Tzokas, N. (1999). The impact of IT on marketing: An evaluation. *Management Decision, 37*(10), 758–766.

Brynjolfsson, E. (1993). The productivity paradox of information technology. *Communications of the ACM, 36*(12), 67–77.

Brynjolfsson, E., & Hitt, L. M. (1998). Beyond the productivity paradox. *Communications of the ACM, 41*(8), 49–55.

Brynjolfsson, E., & Hitt, L. M. (2003). Computing productivity: Firm-level evidence. *The Review of Economics and Statistics, 85*(4), 793–808.

Brynjolfsson, E., & Yang, S. (1996). Information technology and productivity: A review of the literature. In M. V. Zelkowitz (Ed.), *Advances in Computers 43* (pp. 179–241). San Diego, CA: Academic Press.

Buehrer, R. E., Senecal, S., & Pullins, E. B. (2005). Sales force technology usage—reasons, barriers and support: An exploratory investigation. *Industrial Marketing Management, 34*(4), 389–398.

Busbin, J. W., Gross, E. P., & Dillon, T. (1990). Improving spreadsheet control for sales managers through the use of the systems development life cycle. *Journal of Personal Selling & Sales Management, 10*(3), 101–107.

Bush, A. J., Bush, V. D., Orr, L. M., & Rocco, R. A. (2007). Sales technology: Help or hindrance to ethical behaviors and productivity? *Journal of Business Research, 60*(11), 1198–1205.

Bush, A. J., Moore, J. B., & Rocco, R. (2005). Understanding sales force automation outcomes: A managerial perspective. *Industrial Marketing Management, 34*(4), 369–377.

Buttle, F. (2004). *Customer relationship management: Concepts and tools*. Oxford, England: Elsevier Butterworth-Heinemann.

Buttle, F., Ang, L., & Iriana, R. (2006). Sales force automation: Review, critique, research agenda. *International Journal of Manageemnt Reviews, 8*(4), 213–231.

Byrd T., & Marshall, T. (1997). Relating information technology investment to organizational performance: A causal model analysis. *Omega, International Journal of Management Science, 25*(1), 43–56.

Calder, B. J. & Staw, B. M. (1975). Self-perception of intrinsic and extrinsic motivation. *Journal of Personality & Social Psychology, 31*(4), 599–605.

Campbell, T. (1998). Beating the sales force technophobia. *Sales & Marketing Management, 150*(13), 68–72.

Caywood, C. L., & Bauer, C. L. (1986). An electronic bulletin board system for the sales profession: A review and proposal. *Journal of Personal Selling & Sales Management, 6*(3), 85–91.

Chang, W., Park, J. E., Chaiy, S. (in press). How does CRM technology transform into organizational performance? A mediating role of marketing capability. *Journal of Business Research*.

Cho, S. D., & Chang, D. R. (2008). Salesperson's innovation resistance and job satisfaction in intra-organizational diffusion of sales force automation technologies: The case of South Korea. *Industrial Marketing Management, 37*(7), 841–847.

Churchill, G. A., Jr., Ford, N. M., & Walker, O. C., Jr. (1974). Measuring the job satisfaction of industrial salesmen. *Journal of Marketing Research, 11*(3), 254–260.

Collins, R. H. (1984a). Artificial intelligence in personal selling. *Journal of Personal Selling & Sales Management, 4*(1), 58–66.

Collins, R. H. (1984b). Portable computers: Applications to increase salesforce productivity. *Journal of Personal Selling & Sales Management, 4*(2), 75–79.

Collins, R. H. (1985a). Enhancing spreadsheets for increased productivity. *Journal of Personal Selling & Sales Management, 5*(2), 79–81.

Collins, R. H. (1985b). Microcomputer systems to handle sales leads: A key to increased salesforce productivity. *Journal of Personal Selling & Sales Management, 5*(1), 77–80.

Collins, R. H. (1986). Sales training: A microcomputer-based approach. *Journal of Personal Selling & Sales Management, 6*(1), 71–76.

Collins, R. H. (1987). Salesforce support systems: Potential applications to increase productivity. *Journal of the Academy of Marketing Science, 15*(2), 49–54.

Collins, R. H. (1988). Microcomputer applications: The perfect traveling companion: Increasing sales and marketing executive productivity. *Journal of Personal Selling & Sales Management, 8*(1), 67–70.

Collins, R. H., & Mauritson, R. J. (1987). Microcomputer applications: Artificial intelligence in sales forecasting applications. *Journal of Personal Selling & Sales Management, 7*(1), 77–80.

Collins, R. H., Carey, R. F., & Mauritson, R. J. (1987). Microcomputer applications: Maps on a micro: Applications in sales and marketing management. *Journal of Personal Selling & Sales Management, 7*(3), 77–80.

Comer, J. M. (1981/1982). Sales management and the computer: Prospects for the 1980s. *Journal of Personal Selling & Sales Management, 2*(1), 6–9.

Compeau, D. R., & Higgins, C. A. (1995a). Application of social cognitive theory to training for computer skills. *Information Systems Research, 6*(2), 118–143.

Compeau, D. R., & Higgins, C. A. (1995b). Computer self-efficacy: Development of a measure and initial test. *MIS Quarterly, 19*(2), 189–211.

Compton, J. (2003, January). Build or buy? *CRM Magazine, 7*(1), 52–55.

Cooper, R. B., & Zmud, R. W. (1990). Information technology implementation research: A technological diffusion approach. *Management Science, 36*(2), 123–139.

Coppett, J. I., & Voorhees, R. D. (1985). Telemarketing: Supplement to field sales. *Industrial Marketing Management, 14*(3), 213–216.

Cravens, D. W., Grant, K., Ingram, T. N., LaForge, R. W., & Young, C. E. (1992). In search of excellent sales organizations. *European Journal of Marketing, 26*(1), 6–23.

Cravens, D. W., Ingram, T. N., LaForge, R. W., & Young, C. E. (1992). Hallmarks of effective sales organizations. *Marketing Management, 1*(1), 57–66.

CRM Magazine. (2007, October). Statistically speaking. *CRM Magazine, 11*(10), 18.

Cron, W. L., & Sobol, M. G. (1983). The relationship between computerization and performance: A strategy for maximizing the economic benefits of computerization. *Information & Management, 6*(3), 171–181.

Damanpour, F. (1991). Organizational innovation: A meta-analysis of effects of determinants and moderators. *Academy of Management Journal, 34*(3), 555–590.

Davis, F. D. (1986). *A technology acceptance model for empirically testing new end-user information systems: Theory and results* (Unpublished doctoral dissertation). Sloan School of Management, Massachusetts Institute of Technology, Boston.

Davis, F. D. (1989). Perceived usefulness, perceived ease of use, and user acceptance of information technology. *MIS Quarterly, 13*(3), 319–340.

Davis, F. D., Bagozzi, R. P., & Warshaw, P. R. (1989). User acceptance of computer technology: A comparison of two theoretical models. *Management Science, 35*(8), 982–1003.

Davis, F. D., Bagozzi, R. P., & Warshaw, P. R. (1992). Extrinsic and intrinsic motivation to use computers in the workplace. *Journal of Applied Social Psychology, 22*(14), 1111–1132.

Dehning, B., & Richardson, V. (2002). Return on investments in information technology: Beyond the productivity paradox. *Journal of Financial Transfromation, 6,* 83–91.

DeLone, W. H., & McLean, E. R. (1992). Information systems success: The quest for the dependent variable. *Information Systems Research, 3*(1), 60–95.

DeLone, W. H., & McLean, E. R. (2003). The DeLone and McLean model of information systems success: A ten-year update. *Journal of Management Information Systems, 19*(4), 9–30.

Deshpandé, R., Farley, J. U., & Webster, F. E., Jr. (1993). Corporate culture, customer orientation, and innovativeness in Japanese firms: A quadrad analysis. *Journal of Marketing, 57*(1), 23–37.

Dewett, T., & Jones, G. R. (2001). The role of information technology in the organization: A review, model, and assessment. *Journal of Management, 27*(3), 313–346.

Dickie, J. (2006a, July). Demystifying CRM adoption rates. *CRM Magazine, 10*(7), 14.

Dickie, J. (2006b, May). What does CRM really do to help salespeople? *CRM Magazine, 10*(5), 20.

Dishman, P., & Aytes, K. (1996). Exploring group support systems in sales management applications. *Journal of Personal Selling & Sales Management, 16*(1), 65–77.

Drucker, P. F. (1974). *Management, Tasks, Responsibilities, Practices.* London, England: Heinemann.

Dubinsky, A. J., Howell, R. D., Ingram, T. N., & Bellenger, D. N. (1986). Salesforce socialization. *Journal of Marketing, 50*(4), 192–207.

Dugan, S. (1998). Mining the benefits of SFA. *InfoWorld, 20*(40), 74.

Dweck, C. S., & Leggett, E. L. (1988). A social-cognitive approach to motivation and personality. *Psychological Review, 95*(2), 256–273.

Edwards, J. (2007). *Top 9 SFA vendors not named Salesforce.com.* Retrieved December 16, 2009, from http://www.insidecrm.com/features/top-10-sfa -vendors-092607

Engle, R. L., & Barnes, M. L. (2000). Sales force automation usage, effectiveness, and cost-benefit in Germany, England and the United States. *Journal of Business & Industrial Marketing, 15*(4), 216–242.

Erffmeyer, R. C., & Johnson, D. A. (2001). An exploratory study of sales force automation practices: Expectations and realities. *Journal of Personal Selling & Sales Management, 21*(2), 167–175.

Etezadi-Amoli, J., & Farhoomand, A. F. (1996). A structural model of end user computing satisfaction and user performance. *Information & Management, 30*(2), 65–73.

Fishbein, M., & Ajzen, I. (1975). *Belief, attitude, intention and behavior: An introduction to theory and research.* Reading, MA: Addison-Wesley.

Fliegel, F. C., Kivlin, J. E., & Sekhon, G. S. (1967). A cross-national comparison of farmers' perceptions of innovations as related to adoption behavior. *Rural Sociology, 33*(4), 437–449.

Frambach, R. T., & Schillewaert, N. (2002). Organizational innovation adoption: A multi-level framework of determinants and opportunities for future research. *Journal of Business Research, 55*(2), 163–176.

Gartner, Inc. (2009). *Gartner says worldwide CRM market grew 12.5 percent in 2008.* Retrieved December 16, 2009, from http://www.gartner.com/it/page.jsp?id=1074615

Gatignon, H., & Robertson, T. S. (1989). Technology diffusion: An empirical test of competitive effects. *Journal of Marketing, 53*(1), 35–49.

Geiger, S., & Turley, D. (2006). The perceived impact of information technology on salespeople's rational competencies. *Journal of Marketing Management, 22*(7), 827–851.

Gelderman, M. (1998). The relation between user satisfaction, usage of information systems, and performance. *Information & Management, 34*(1), 11–18.

Gohmann, S. F., Barker, R. M., Faulds, D. J., & Guan, J. (2005). Sales force automation, perceived information accuracy and user satisfaction. *Journal of Business and Industrial Marketing, 20*(1), 23–32.

Gohmann, S. F., Guan, J., Barker, R. M. & Faulds, D. J. (2005). Perceptions of sales force automation: differences between sales force and management. *Industrial Marketing Management, 34*(4), 337–343.

Golany, B., & Tamir, E. (1995). Evaluating efficiency-effectiveness-equality trade-offs: A data-envelopment analysis approach. *Management Science, 41*(7), 1172–1184.

Goldenberg, B. (2006, April). Executive support: the most important CRM success factor. *CRM Magazine, 10*(4), 18.

Good, D. J., & Stone, R. W. (2000). The impact of computerization on marketing performance. *Journal of Business and Industrial Marketing, 15*(1), 34–56.

Goodhue, D. L., & Thompson, R. L. (1995). Task-technology fit and individual performance. *MIS Quarterly, 19*(2), 213–233.

Goodhue, D. L., Klein, B. D., & March, S. T. (2000). User evaluations of IS as surrogates for objective performance. *Information & Management, 38*(2), 87–101.

Gunasekaran, A., Love, P. E. D., Rahimi, F., & Miele, R. (2001). A model for investment justification in information technology projects. *International Journal of Information Management, 21*(5), 349–364.

Gupta, S., & Zeithaml, V. (2006). Customer metrics and their impact on financial performance. *Marketing Science, 25*(6), 687–717.

Hartwick, J., & Barki, H. (1994). Explaining the role of user participation in information system use. *Management Science, 40*(4), 440–465.

Hendricks, K. B., Singhal, V. R., & Stratman, J. K. (2007). The impact of enterprise systems on corporate performance: A study of ERP, SCM, and CRM system implementations. *Journal of Operations Management, 25*(1), 65–82.

Hennessey, H. D. (1988). Microcomputer applications: Accelerating the salesperson learning curve. *Journal of Personal Selling & Sales Management, 8*(3), 77–82.

Heschel, M. S. (1977). Effective sales territory development. *Journal of Marketing, 41*(2), 39–43.

Higgins, L. F., McIntyre, S. C., & Raine, C. G. (1991). Design of global information systems. *Journal of Business and Industrial Marketing, 6*(3/4), 49–58.

Hill, N. C., & Swenson, M. J. (1994). The impact of electronic data interchange on the sales function. *Journal of Personal Selling & Sales Management, 14*(3), 79–87.

Hise, R. T., & Reid, E. L. (1994). Improving the performance of the industrial salesforce in the 1990s. *Industrial Marketing Management, 23*(4), 73–79.

Hitt, L., & Brynjolfsson, E. (1996). Productivity, business profitability, and consumer surplus: Three different measures of information technology values. *MIS Quarterly, 20*(2), 21–142.

Hofstede, G. (1980). *Culture's Consequences: International Differences in Work-Related Values.* Beverly Hills, CA: Sage.

Homburg, C., Wieseke, J., & Kuehnl, C. (in press). Social influence on salespeople's adoption of sales technology: A multilevel analysis. *Journal of the Academy of Marketing Science.*

Honeycutt, E. D., Jr., McCarty, T., & Howe, V. (1993). Sales technology applications: Self-paced video enhanced training: A case study. *Journal of Personal Selling & Sales Management, 13*(1), 73–79.

Honeycutt, E., D, Jr., Thelen, T., Thelen, S. T., & Hodge, S. K. (2005). Impediments to sales force automation. *Industrial Marketing Management, 34*(4), 313–322.

Hughes, D. G. (1983). Computerized sales management. *Harvard Business Review, 61*(2), 102–112.

Hunter, G. K., & Perreault, W. D. (2006). Sales technology orientation, information effectiveness, and sales performance. *Journal of Personal Selling and Sales Management, 36*(2), 95–113.

Hunter, G. K., & Perreault, W. D. (2007). Making sales technology effective. *Journal of Marketing, 71*(1), 16–34.

Iacovou, C. L., Benbasat, I., & Dexter, A. S. (1995). Electronic data interchange and small organisations: Adoption and impact of technology. *MIS Quarterly, 19*(4), 465–485.

Igbaria, M., & Tan, M. (1997). The consequences of the information technology acceptance on subsequent individual performance. *Information & Management, 32*(3), 113–121.

Jarvenpaa, S. L., & Ives, B. (1991). Executive involvement and participation in the management of information technology. *MIS Quarterly, 15*(2), 205–227.

Jasperson, J., Carter, P. E., & Zmud, R. W. (2005). A comprehensive conceptualization of post-adoptive behaviors associated with information technology enabled work systems. *MIS Quarterly, 29*(3), 525–557.

Jaworski, B., & Kohli, A. (1993). Market orientation: Antecedents and consequences. *Journal of Marketing, 57*(3), 53–70.

Jayachandran, S., Sharma, S., Kaufman, P., & Raman, P. (2005). The role of relational information processes and technology use in customer relationship management. *Journal of Marketing, 69*(4), 177–192.

Jelinek, R., Ahearne, M., Mathieu, J., & Schillewaert, N. (2006). A longitudinal examination of individual, organizational, and contextual factors on sales technology adoption and job performance. *Journal of Marketing Theory & Practice, 14*(1), 7–23.

Jimmieson, N. L., Peach, M., & White, K. M. (2008). Utilizing the theory of planned behavior to inform change management: An investigation of employee intentions to support organizational change. *Journal of Applied Behavioral Science, 44*(2), 237–262.

Johannessen, J. A., Olaisen, J., & Olsen, B. (1999). Strategic use of information technology for increased innovation and performance. *Information Management and Computer Security, 7*(1), 5–22.

Johnson, D. S., & Bharadwaj, S. (2005). Digitization of selling activity and sales force performance: An empirical investigation. *Journal of the Academy of Marketing Science, 33*(1), 3–18.

Jones, E., Sundaram, S., & Chin, W. (2002). Factors leading to sales force automation use: A longitudinal analysis. *Journal of Personal Selling and Sales Management, 1*(3), 145–156.

Karahanna, E., Straub, D. W., & Chervany, N. L. (1999). Information technology adoption across time: A cross-sectional comparison of pre-adoption and post-adoption beliefs. *MIS Quarterly, 23*(2), 183–213.

Keillor, B. D., Bashaw, E. R., & Pettijohn, C. E. (1997). Salesforce automation issues prior to implementation: The relationship between attitudes toward technology, experience, and productivity. *Journal of Business & Industrial Marketing, 12*(3/4), 209–219.

Kim, N., & Srivastava, R. K. (1998). Managing intraorganizational diffusion of technological innovations. *Industrial Marketing Management, 27*(3), 229–246.

King, W. R., & He, J. (2006). A meta-analysis of the technology acceptance model. *Information & Management, 43*(6), 740–755.

Kirpalani, V. H., & Shapiro, S. S. (1973). Financial dimensions of marketing management. *Journal of Marketing, 37*(3), 40–47.

Kivijärvi, H., & Saarinen, T. (1995). Investment in information systems and the financial performance of the firm. *Information & Management, 28*(2), 143–163.

Klein K. J., Conn, A. B., & Sorra, J. S. (2001). Implementing computerized technology: An organizational analysis. *Journal of Applied Psychology, 86*(5), 811–824.

Klein, K. J., & Sorra, J. S. (1996). The challenge of innovation implementation. *Academy of Management Review, 21*(4), 1055–1080.

Ko, D. G., & Dennis, A. R. (2004). Sales force automation and sales performance: Do experience and expertise matter? *Journal of Personal Selling & Sales Management, 24*(4), 311–322.

Kohli, R., & Devaraj, S. (2003). Measuring information technology payoff: A meta-analysis of structural variables in firm-level empirical research. *Information Systems Research, 14*(2), 127–145.

Krasnikov, A., Jayachandran, S., & Kumar, V. (2009). The impact of CRM implementation on cost and profit efficiencies: Evidence from the U.S. commercial banking industry. *Journal of Marketing, 73*(6), 61–76.

Krigsman, M. (2009). *CRM failure rates: 2001–2009.* Retrieved December 12, 2009, from http://blogs.zdnet.com/projectfailures/?p=4967

Kwahk, K., & Lee, J. (2008). The role of readiness for change in ERP implementation: Theoretical bases and empirical validation. *Information & Management, 45*(7), 474–481.

Landry, T. D., Arnold, T. J., & Arndt, A. (2005). A compendium of sales-related literature in customer relationship management: Processes and technologies with managerial implications. *Journal of Personal Selling & Sales Management, 25*(3), 231–251.

Lapierre, J., & Denier, A. (2005). ICT adoption and moderating effects of institutional factors on salesperson's communication effectiveness: A contingency study in high-tech industries. *Technovation, 25*(8), 909–927.

Lee, S. C. (2001). Modeling the business value of information technology. *Information & Management, 39*(3), 191–210.

Lewin, K. (1952). Group decision and social change. In T. Newcomb & E. Hartley (Eds.), *Readings in social psychology* (pp. 459–473). New York, NY: Henry Holt.

Li, M., & Ye, L. R. (1999). Information technology and firm performance: Linking with environmental, strategic and managerial contexts. *Information & Management, 35*(1), 43–51.

Lodish, L. M. (1971). CALLPLAN: An interactive salesman's call planning system. *Management Science, 18*(4), 25–40.

Long, M. M., Tellefsen, T., & Lichtenthal, D. J. (2007). Internet integration into the industrial selling process: A step-by-step approach. *Industrial Marketing Management, 36*(5), 676–689.

Lucas, H. C., Jr. (1975). Performance and the use of an information system. *Management Science, 21*(8), 908–919.

Mahmood, M. A., Burn, J. M., Gemoets, L. A., & Jacquez, C. (2000). Variables affecting information technology end-user satisfaction: A meta-analysis of the empirical literature. *International Journal of Human-Computer Studies, 52*(4), 751–771.

Mallin, M. L., & DelVecchio, S. K. (2008). Salesforce automation tool selectivity: An agency theory perspective. *Journal of Business & Industrial Marketing, 23*(7), 486–496.

Manssen, B. L. (1990). Using PCs to automate and innovate marketing activities. *Industrial Marketing Management, 19*(3), 209–213.

Marinova, D., Ye, J., & Singh, J. (2008). Do frontline mechanisms matter? Impact of quality and productivity orientations on unit revenue, efficiency, and customer satisfaction. *Journal of Marketing, 72*(2), 28–45.

Marshall, G. W., Moncrief, W. C., & Lassk, F. G. (1999). The current state of sales force activities. *Industrial Marketing Management, 28*(1), 87–98.

Marshall, J. J., & Vredenburg, H. (1988). Successfully using telemarketing in industrial sales. *Industrial Marketing Management, 17*(1), 5–22.

Martin, W. S., & Collins, B. S. (1991). Interactive video technology in sales training: A case study. *Journal of Personal Selling & Sales Management, 11*(3), 61–66.

Mathieson, K. (1991). Predicting user intentions: Comparing the technology acceptance model with the theory of planned behavior. *Information Systems Research, 2*(3), 173–191.

Mathieu, J., Ahearne, M., & Taylor, S. R. (2007). A longitudinal cross-level model of leader and salesperson influences on sales force technology use and performance. *Journal of Applied Psychology, 92*(2), 528–537.

McKay, L. (2009, July). Simplementation: 10 tips to smooth your CRM initiative. *CRM Magazine, 13*(7), 28–32.

McKee, D., & Varadarajan, P. R. (1995). Special issue on sustainable competitive advantage. *Journal of Business Research, 33*(2), 91–101.

Moncrief, W. C., III, & Cravens, D. W. (1999). Technology and the changing marketing world. *Marketing Intelligence & Planning, 17*(7), 329–332.

Moncrief, W. C., III, Lamb, C. W., Jr., & McKay, J. (1991). Laptop computers in industrial sales. *Industrial Marketing Management, 20*(4), 279–285.

Moncrief, W. C., III, Shipp, S. H., Lamb, C. W., Jr., & Cravens, D. W. (1989). Examining the roles of telemarketing in selling strategy. *Journal of Personal Selling & Sales Management, 9*(3), 1–12.

Moore, G. C., & Benbasat, I. (1991). Development of an instrument to measure the perceptions of adopting an information technology innovation. *Information Systems Research, 2*(3), 192–222.

Morgan, A. J., & Inks, S. A. (2001). Technology and the sales force: Increasing acceptance of sales force automation. *Industrial Marketing Management, 30*(5), 463–472.

Moriarty, R. T., & Swartz, G. S. (1989). Automation to boost sales and marketing. *Harvard Business Review, 67*(1), 100–109.

Morris, M. G., & Venkatesh, V. (2000). Age differences in technology adoption decisions: Implications of a changing workforce. *Personnel Psychology, 53*(2), 375–403.

Moutot, J. M., & Bascoul, G. (2008). Effects of sales force automation use on sales force activities and customer relationship management processes. *Journal of Personal Selling & Sales Management, 28*(2), 167–184.

Mulki, J. P., Locander, W. B., Marshall, G. W., Harris, E. G., & Hensel, J. (2008). Workplace isolation, salesperson commitment, and job performance. *Journal of Personal Selling & Sales Management, 28*(1), 67–78.

Ostroff, C., & Schmitt, N. (1993). Configurations of organizational effectiveness and efficiency. *Academy of Management Journal, 36*(6), 1345–1361.

Ostrow, P. (2008). *Mobile CRM: Empowering the 24/7 road warrior.* Retrieved December 20, 2009, from http://www.crmbuyer.com/story/61797.html

Pae, J. H., Kim, N., Han, J. K., & Yip, L. (2002). Managing intraorganizational diffusion of innovations: Impact of buying center dynamics and environments. *Industrial Marketing Management, 31*(8), 719–726.

Palmatier, R. W., Scheer, L. K., & Steenkamp, J. B. E. M. (2007). Customer loyalty to whom? Managing the benefits and risks of salesperson-owned loyalty. *Journal of Marketing Research, 44*(2), 185–199.

Papastathopoulou, P., Avlonitis, G. J., & Panagopoulos, N. G. (2007). Intraorganizational information and communication technology diffusion: Implications for industrial sellers and buyers. *Industrial Marketing Management, 36*(3), 322–336.

Park, J. E., Kim, J., Dubinsky, A. J., & Lee, H. (in press) How does sales force automation influence relationship quality and performance? The mediating roles of learning and selling behaviors. *Industrial Marketing Management.*

Parthasarathy, M., & Sohi, R. S. (1997). Salesforce automation and the adoption of technological innovations by salespeople: Theory and implications. *Journal of Business and Industrial Marketing, 12*(3/4), 196–208

Pauwels, K., Ambler, T., Clark, B. H., LaPointe, P., Reibstein, D., Skiera, B., Wierenga, B., & Wiesel, T. (2009). Dashboards as a service: Why, what, how, and what research is needed? *Journal of Service Research. 12*(2), 175–189.

Pavlou, P. A. (2002). Consumer acceptance of electronic commerce: Integrating trust and risk with the technology acceptance model. *International Journal of Electronic Commerce, 7*(3), 69–103.

Payne, A., & Frow, P. (2005). A strategic framework for customer relationship management. *Journal of Marketing, 69*(4), 167–176.

Petouhoff, N. (2006, April). The scientific reason for CRM failure. *CRM Magazine, 10*(4), 48.

Petter, S., & McLean, E. R. (2009). A meta-analytic assessment of the DeLone and McLean IS success model: An examination of IS success at the individual level. *Information & Management, 46*(3), 159–166.

Plouffe, C. R., Williams, B. C., & Leigh, T. W. (2004). Who's on first? Stakeholder differences in customer relationship management and the elusive notion of "shared understanding." *Journal of Personal Selling & Sales Management, 24*(4), 323–338.

Porter, M. E. (1985). *Competitive strategy: Creating and sustaining superior performance.* New York, NY: Free Press.

Powell, T. C., & Dent-Micallef, A. (1997). Information technology as competitive advantage: The role of human, business, and technology resources. *Strategic Management Journal, 18*(5), 375–405.

Prattipati, S. N., & Mensah, M. O. (1997). Information systems variables and management productivity. *Information & Management, 33*(1), 33–43.

Pullig, C., Maxham, J. G., III, & Hair, J. F., Jr. (2002). Salesforce automation systems: An exploratory examination of organizational factors associated with effective implementation and salesforce productivity. *Journal of Business Research, 55*(5), 401–415.

Quinn, R. F., & Rohrbaugh, J. (1981). A competing values approach to organizational effectiveness. *Public Productivity Review, 5*(2), 122–140.

Radcliffe, J. (2001). *Eight building blocks of CRM: A framework for success.* Retrieved December 17, 2009, from http://www.gartner.com/resources/103200/103204/103204.pdf

Raghunathan, S., & Yeh, A. B. (2001). Beyond EDI: Impact of continuous replenishment program (CRP) between a manufacturer and its retailers. *Information Systems Research, 12*(4), 406–419.

Raman, P., Wittmann, M., & Rauseo, N. (2006). Leveraging CRM for sales: The role of organizational capabilities in successful CRM implementation. *Journal of Personal Selling & Sales Management, 26*(1), 39–53.

Rangarajan, D., Jones, E., & Chin, W. (2005). Impact of sales force automation on technology-related stress, effort, and technology usage among salespeople. *Industrial Marketing Management, 34*(4), 345–354.

Rapp, A., Agnihotri, R., & Forbes, L. P. (2008). The sales force technology-performance chain: The role of adaptive selling and effort. *Journal of Personal Selling & Sales Management, 28*(4), 335–350.

Rasmusson, E. (1999, March). The 5 steps to successful sales force automation. *Sales & Marketing Management, 151*(3), 34–39.

Reinartz, W., Krafft, M., & Hoyer, W. D. (2004). The customer relationship management process: Its measurement and impact on performance. *Journal of Marketing Research, 41*(3), 293–305.

Richard, J. E., Thirkell, P. C., & Huff, S. L. (2007). An examination of customer relationship management (CRM) technology adoption and its impact on business-to-business customer relationship. *Total Quality Management, 18*(8), 927–945.

Rigby, D. K., Reichheld, F. F., & Schefter, P. (2002). Avoid the four perils of CRM. *Harvard Business Review, 80*(2), 101–109.

Rivers, M. L., & Dart, J. (1999). The acquisition and use of sales force automation by mid-sized manufacturers. *Journal of Personal Selling & Sales Management, 19*(2), 59–73.

Robertson, T. S., & Gatignon, H. (1986), Competitive effects on technology diffusion. *Journal of Marketing, 50*(3), 1–12.

Robinson, L., Jr., Marshall, G. W., & Stamps, M. B. (2005a). An empirical investigation of technology acceptance in a field sales force setting. *Industrial Marketing Management, 34*(4), 407–415.

Robinson, L., Jr., Marshall, G. W., & Stamps, M. B. (2005b). Sales force use of technology: Antecedents to technology acceptance. *Journal of Business Research, 58*(12), 1623–1631.

Rogers, E. M. (1983). *Diffusion of innovations* (3rd ed.). New York, NY: Free Press.

Rogers, E. M. (1995). *Diffusion of innovations* (4th ed.). New York, NY: Free Press.

Rogers, E. M., & Shoemaker, P. (1971). *Communication of innovations.* New York, NY: Free Press.

Rothman, J. (1974). *Planning and organizing for social change: Action principles from social science research.* New York, NY: Columbia University Press.

Rust, R. T., Ambler, T., Carpenter, G. S., Kumar, V., & Srivastava, R. K. (2004). Measuring marketing productivity: Current knowledge and future directions. *Journal of Marketing, 68*(4), 76–89.

Samli, C. A., Wills, J. R., Jr., & Herbig, P. (1997). The information superhighway goes international: Implications for industrial sales transactions. *Industrial Marketing Management, 26*(1), 51–58.

Schepers, J., & Wetzels, M. (2007). A meta-analysis of the technology acceptance model: Investigating subjective norm and moderation effects. *Information & Management, 44*(1), 90–103.

Schillewaert, N., Ahearne, M. J., Frambach, R. T., & Moenaert, R. K. (2000). *The acceptance of information technology in the sales force* (No. ISBM Report 15-2000). University Park: Pennsylvania State University, Institute for the Study of Business Markets.

Schillewaert, N., Ahearne, M. J., Frambach, R. T., & Moenaert, R. K. (2005). The adoption of information technology in the sales force. *Industrial Marketing Management, 34*(4), 323–336.

Seiders, K., Voss, G. B., Grewal, D., & Godfrey, A. L. (2005). Do satisfied customers buy more? Examining moderating influences in a retailing context. *Journal of Marketing, 69*(4), 26–43.

Senecal, S., Pullins, E. B., & Buehrer, R. E. (2007). The extent of technology usage and salespeople: An exploratory investigation. *Journal of Business & Industrial Marketing, 22*(1), 52–61.

Sheth, J. N., & Sisodia, R. S. (2002). Marketing productivity: Issues and analysis. *Journal of Business Research, 55*(5), 349–362.

Shih, C. F., & Venkatesh, A. (2004). Beyond adoption: Development and application of a use-diffusion model. *Journal of Marketing, 68*(1), 59–72.

Singh, J. (1998). Striking a balance in boundary-spanning positions: An investigation of some unconventional influences of role stressors and job characteristics on job outcomes of salespeople. *Journal of Marketing, 62*(3), 69–86.

Skiera, B., & Albers, S. (1998). COSTA: Contribution optimizing sales territory alignment. *Marketing Science, 17*(3), 196–213.

Speier, C., & Venkatesh, V. (2002). The hidden minefields in the adoption of sales force automation technologies. *Journal of Marketing, 66,* 98–111.

Srivastava, R. K., Shervani, T. A., & Fahey, L. (1999). Marketing, business processes, and shareholder value: An organizationally embedded view of marketing activities and the discipline of marketing. [Special issue]. *Journal of Marketing, 63,* 168–179.

Steenkamp, J. B. E. M., Hofstede, F. T., & Wedel, M. (1999). A cross-national investigation into the individual and national-cultural antecedents of consumer innovativeness. *Journal of Marketing, 63*(2), 55–69.

Steinberg, M., & Plank, R. E. (1987). Expert systems: The integrative sales management tool of the future. *Journal of the Academy of Marketing Science, 15*(2), 55–62.

Stevenson, T. H., Plath, D. A., & Bush, C. M. (1990). Using expert systems in industrial marketing. *Industrial Marketing Management, 19*(3), 243–249.

Stratopoulos, T., & Dehning, B. (2000). Does successful investment in information technology solve the productivity paradox? *Information & Management, 38*(2), 103–117.

Straub, D., Limayem, M., & Karahanna-Evaristo, E. (1995). Measuring system usage: Implications for IS theory testing. *Management Science, 14*(8), 1328–1342.

Strite, M. (2006). Culture as an explanation of technology acceptance differences: An empirical investigation of Chinese and US users. *Australasian Journal of Information Systems, 14*(1), 5–26.

Strout, E. (1999). Charting a course. *Sales & Marketing Management, 151*(8), 46–53.

Sujan, H., Weitz, B. A., & Kumar, N. (1994). Learning orientation, working smart, and effective selling. *Journal of Marketing, 58*(3), 39–52.

Sun, H., &. Zhang, P. (2006). The role of moderating factors in user technology acceptance. *International Journal of Human-Computer Studies, 64*(2), 53–78.

Sundaram, S., Schwarz, A., Jones, E., & Chin, W. W. (2007). Technology use on the front line: How information technology enhances individual performance. *Journal of the Academy of Marketing Science, 35*(1), 101–112.

Sviokla, J. J. (1996). Knowledge workers and radically new technology. *Sloan Management Review, 37*(4), 25–40.

Swenson, M. J., & Parrella, A. (1992). Cellular telephones and the national sales force. *Journal of Personal Selling & Sales Management, 12*(4), 67–74.

Tanner, J. F., Jr., Ahearne, M., Leigh, T. W., Mason, C. H., & Moncrief, W. C. (2005). CRM in sales-intensive organizations: A review and future directions. *Journal of Personal Selling & Sales Management, 25*(2), 169–180.

Tanner, J. F., Jr., & Shipp, S. (2005). Sales technology within the salesperson's relationships: A research agenda. *Industrial Marketing Management, 34*(4), 305–312.

Taylor, S., & Todd, P. A. (1995a). Assessing IT usage: The role of prior experience. *MIS Quarterly, 19*(2), 561–570.

Taylor, S., & Todd, P. A. (1995b). Understanding information technology usage: A test of competing models. *Information Systems Research, 6*(4), 144–176.

Teo, T. S. H., & Wong, P. K. (1998). An empirical study of the performance impact of computerization in the retail industry. *Omega, 26*(5), 611–621.

Thompson, R. L., Higgins, C. A., & Howell, J. M. (1991). Personal computing: Toward a conceptual model of utilization. *MIS Quarterly, 15*(1), 124–143.

Thompson, R. L., Higgins, C. A., & Howell, J. M. (1994). Influence of experience on personal computer utilization: Testing a conceptual model. *Journal of Management Information Systems, 11*(1), 167–187.

Tornatzky, L. G., & Klein, R. J. (1982). Innovation characteristics and innovation adoption implementation: A meta-analysis of findings. *IEEE Transactions on Engineering Management, 29*(1), 28–45.

Triandis, H. C. (1980). Values, attitudes, and interpersonal behavior. In H. Howe & M. Page (Eds.), *Nebraska Symposium on Motivation, 1979: Beliefs, Attitudes, and Values* (pp. 195–260). Lincoln, NE: University of Nebraska Press.

Veiga, J. F., Floyd, S., & Dechant, K. (2001). Towards modeling the effects of national culture on IT implementation and acceptance. *Journal of Information Technology, 16*(3), 145–158.

Venkatesh, V., & Davis, F. D. (2000). A theoretical extension of the technology acceptance model: Four longitudinal field studies. *Management Science, 46*(2), 186–204.

Venkatesh, V., & Morris, M. G. (2000). Why don't men ever stop to ask for directions? Gender, social influence, and their role in technology acceptance and usage behavior. *MIS Quarterly, 24*(1), 115–139.

Venkatesh, V., Morris, M. G., & Ackerman, P. L. (2000). A longitudinal field investigation of gender differences in individual technology adoption decision making processes. *Organizational Behavior and Human Decision Processes, 83*(1), 33–60.

Venkatesh, V., Morris, M. G., Davis, G. B., & Davis, F. D. (2003). User acceptance of information technology: Toward a unified view. *MIS Quarterly, 27*(3), 425–478.

Walton, R. E., & Dutton, J. M. (1969). The management of interdepartment conflict: A model and review. *Administrative Science Quarterly, 14*(1), 73–84.

Webster, J., & Martocchio, J. J. (1992). Microcomputer playfulness: Development of a measure with workplace implications. *MIS Quarterly, 16*(2), 201–226.

Wedell, A., & Hempeck, D. (1987). Sales force automation: Here and now. *Journal of Personal Selling & Sales Management, 7*(2), 11–16.

Widmier, S. M., Jackson, D. W., Jr., & McCabe, D. B. (2002). Infusing technology into personal selling. *Journal of Personal Selling & Sales Management, 22*(3), 189–198.

Zablah, A. R., Bellenger, D. N., & Johnston, W. J. (2004a). An evaluation of divergent perspectives on customer relationship management: Towards a common understanding of an emerging phenomenon. *Industrial Marketing Management, 33*(6), 475–489.

Zablah, A. R., Bellenger, D. N., & Johnston, W. J. (2004b). Customer relationship management implementation gaps. *Journal of Personal Selling & Sales Management, 24*(4), 279–295.

Zaltman, G., Duncan, R., & Holbek, J. (1973). *Innovations and organizations.* New York, NY: John Wiley.

Zmud, R. W. (1982). Diffusion of modern software practices: Influence of centralization and formalization. *Management Science, 28*(12), 1421–1431.

Zmud, R. W., & Apple, L. (1992). Measuring technology incorporation/infusion. *Journal of Product Innovation Management, 9*(2), 148–155.

Index

N
NetSuite, Inc., 21
notebook computers, 12

O
Oracle, 21
organizational influences, 61–69,
    62*t*–63*t*

P
performance implications of sales
    technology, 77–95
Perreault, W. D., 6, 91*t*
person-technology fit, 51*t*, 53
portable computers, 7
productivity paradox, information
    technology (IT), 77, 78–81

R
Rangarajan, D., 61
Rapp, A., 6, 20, 94*t*
return on sales technology investment
    (ROSTI), 97
    calculating, 105–14, 107*f*, 112*t*,
        114*t*
RightNow Technologies, Inc., 21
road map for success, 115–40,
    132*t*–133*t*
Rogers, E., 24
Rust, R. T., 107

S
Salesboom.com, Inc., 21
sales force automation (SFA), 1–6, 3*t*,
    4*t*, 13, 21, 24, 34, 50, 57, 64,
    85, 93*t*, 107, 129
Salesforce.com, Inc., 21
sales force efficiency and productiv-
    ity, 4
SalesNexus LLC, 21
salesperson-centric technologies, 20
Salesperson-Customer Interface (SCI)
    Technology Continuum, 20
salesperson-customer shared technolo-
    gies, 21

salesperson performance, sales tech-
    nology impact, 85–89
salesperson-specific technologies, 20
SalesPush Limited, 21
sales technologies, 1–22, 3*t*, 4*t*, 9*t*–11*t*
    B2B selling context, 15–16
    in business-to-consumer selling
        context, 20–21
    defining, 1–6
    history and evolution, 6–21, 7*f*
    impact on salesperson performance,
        85–89
    implementation process, 23–48
    literature review, 90*t*–95*t*
    market, 21
    measuring impact, 97–114
    for supporting company-customer
        interface activities, 16–18
    for supporting sales force activities,
        19–20
    for supporting sales management
        activities, 18–19
    types and uses, 15–21, 16*f*
    vendors, 21
SAP AG, 21
Schwarz, A., 26*t*, 27, 95*t*
SFA. *See* sales force automation (SFA)
Shervani, T. A., 5
social cognitive model of technology
    usage (SCMTU), 44–45, 44*t*
social media, 14
Sorra, J. S., 26*t*, 29, 63, 98
Speier, C., 53
spreadsheet analysis, 8
Srivastava, R. K., 5
SugarCRM, Inc., 21
Sundaram, S., 27
supporting
    company-customer interface activi-
        ties, 16–18
    sales force activities, 19–20
    sales management activities, 17*t*,
        18–19
system characteristics, 50–54, 51*t*

T
task-technology fit (TTF), 71